ECONOMIZING ABUNDANCE

BOOKS BY ROBERT THEOBALD
    The Rich and the Poor (1960)
    The Challenge of Abundance (1961)
    Profit Potential in the Developing Countries (1962)
    Free Men and Free Markets (1963)
    Business Potential in the European Common Market (1963)
    The Guaranteed Income, ed. (1966)
    Social Policies for America in the Seventies, ed. (1968)
    An Alternative Future for America II (1970)
    Bobbs-Merrill Dialogue Series, ed.
    Habit and Habitat (1972)
    Futures Conditional (1972)
    Teg's 1994 (1972)
    Economizing Abundance (1970, 1972)
    Middle Class Support (1968, 1972)

ECONOMIZING ABUNDANCE:
A Non-Inflationary Future

Robert Theobald

THE SWALLOW PRESS INC.
CHICAGO

Copyright © 1970 by Pitman Publishing Corporation
All rights reserved
Printed in the United States of America

Published by
The Swallow Press Incorporated
1139 South Wabash Avenue
Chicago, Illinois 60605

This book is printed on 100% recycled paper.

ISBN 0-8040-0611-3
Library of Congress Catalog Card Number 79-125096

11-28-73

This book was originally published in a clothbound edition under the title, *The Economics of Abundance: A Non-Inflationary Future,* in 1970 by The Pitman Publishing Corporation.

To Lynn

CONTENTS

Introduction, 3

ECONOMIC THEORY—PAST, PRESENT, and FUTURE

A Brief History of Recent Economic Thought, 15
A New Theoretical Understanding, 31
Growth in Supply, 51
Growth in Demand, 63

INTERMISSION The Issues Defined, 77

ECONOMIC POLICIES IN THE SEVENTIES

Policy Measures to Change the Distribution of Resources, 87
Other Policy Measures: Labor-Management, Capital, Taxation, 99
The End of Inflation, 113
Short-Run Economic Issues, 127

EPILOGUE Socioeconomic Problem/Possibilities, 139

ACKNOWLEDGMENTS

As always, this book would not have been finished without the contribution of my wife. Her help ranges from the creation of new conceptualizations to the correction of muddy thinking and the elimination of incorrect grammar.

In addition, I must state my debt to Professor Goodwin, who led me to see that the whole structure of economics was open to challenge, that there were no certainties, and that as conditions changed economics also had to change if it was to remain valid.

INTRODUCTION

It is now clear that the policies of the Nixon Administration have created a recession. The only remaining question is whether the recession will develop into a disaster.

A combination of rising rates of unemployment, high rates of inflation, and a decline in real Gross National Product is a politician's nightmare. Something has obviously gone seriously wrong with President Nixon's carefully planned postelection economic strategy. This aimed to control inflation during 1969 by carefully slowing the economy and then insuring a rapid rate of growth and relatively stable prices in 1970. Voters were intended to go to the polls in a satisfied mood both because of the successful movement toward stable prices as well as the resumption of growth in their income.

This highly desirable pattern has failed to develop. The Nixon Administration now confronts a situation where the "average voter" is likely to be angry about economic matters and therefore against the party in power. This book will show what went wrong in 1969 and why economic calculations will continue to go wrong until economists change their thinking fundamentally. We shall discover that the United States, and indeed the whole Western World, must change their economic theories if they are to take advantage of the potential which the new technologies are creating to provide every human being with a decent standard of living.

It can be expected that considerable efforts will be made to prevent us from examining the fundamental realities of our present situation. For example, it is inevitable that the Nixon Administration will try to improve the *apparent* economic situation before the 1972 elections. It is also inevitable that the Administration will launch propaganda barrages designed to convince the society that, although its previous programs have been unsuccessful, its new programs *will* be satisfactory. For example, it seems probable that the Nixon Administration will try to insure the availability of more funds by 1971. This will not, however, solve the present basic difficulties. It will only put off the date at which the culture will be forced to face up to its real economic problems.

We must learn immediately that politically motivated cosmetic activities are no longer adequate in our situation. We are already living in a new economic system. Unfortunately, as we enter the seventies, there is still no evidence of fundamental change in direction. Economic growth is not being significantly redirected toward socially and ecologically desirable ends, evidence of economic and societal imbalance is increasingly obvious, and there is a continuously widening gap between the resources available to those with power and those with no access to power.

Failure to develop new economic theory and new economic practice in the immediate future will lead to crises far more serious than those of the thirties. However, the discipline of economics seems determined to retain its claim to the title "the dismal science." Economists refuse to admit that mankind's increasing knowledge and skills have created a situation in which it can produce an abundance of material goods and services using limited quantities of labor. Despite rapidly changing circumstances and increasingly sophisticated consumers, economists continue to think and act as though mankind were still controlled by the overall scarcity-industrial pattern that existed in the nineteenth century. They have not enlarged their discipline to include the new patterns of specific scarcities within general abundance.

Our present economic problem is that our basic economic goals are in conflict: full employment and price stability have become incompatible within an economy oriented toward economic growth. The history of this development is clearly traceable: the break comes at the time when neoclassical free-market policies were replaced by neo-Keynesian policies of economic management. The self-interest of workers always dictated that they attempt to raise their income levels as rapidly as possible. However, such attempts were always modified by the knowledge that increases in wages raise costs—and that if costs were raised too far, firms and industries might be priced out of the market. With the full introduction of neo-Keynesian economic management in America in the sixties, this constraint has largely disappeared. Economic theory now holds that the government is responsible for manipulating the economy so that there are jobs for all. In a neo-Keynesian world, the economy is so ordered that higher wages and prices do not normally result in loss of jobs or orders but only in general inflation.

Price stability, which is basic to the effective functioning of any economic system, is a direct casualty of the neo-Keynesian economic policies presently being practiced. *The full understanding of the implications of neo-Keynesian policies by those involved in making economic decisions insures, in itself, that it will be impossible to continue these policies.* This highly unpalatable truth has been inherent in most recent economic analyses of current events, but we have not yet been willing to bring the issue out into the open.

Governments controlling modern Western economic systems face an insoluble dilemma. The inflation which has resulted from past efforts of various groups to gain resources can be prevented from developing further only if *all* those involved see penalties *for themselves* in continuing to demand larger wage, salary, and price increases than are justified by productivity increases. Unfortunately, however, once the expectation of inflation has developed, people believe that they will necessarily benefit from rapid rises in wages, salaries, and prices, and will certainly suffer if they fail to attain them. The consequent pattern of expectations and decisions can be broken only if a recession is created, with consequent high levels of unemployment. This, in effect, would end neo-Keynesianism, which is pledged to continue full employment. If, on the other hand, the government continues neo-Keynesianism and remains pledged to full employment, then inflationary expectations and conditions will necessarily worsen.

As we look ahead, it seems that we are trapped in a triangle of our basic economic goals: we cannot obtain economic growth, full employment, and price stability. If we wish to insure price stability, we must tolerate ever-higher levels of unemployment. If we want to insure lower levels of unemployment, we must tolerate ever-higher rates of inflation. So long as we continue to practice neo-Keynesian economics, the situation will continue to deteriorate.

The experience of Great Britain, which adopted neo-Keynesian policies immediately after World War II, proves this point clearly. The key dilemma which has hamstrung policy makers in Great Britain for almost twenty-five years has been the continuing combined commitment to price stability and low unemployment. As we enter the seventies, the United States, which has so far been sufficiently disciplined in its labor-management relations to avoid the worst consequences of the neo-Keynesian dilemma, is facing its reality.

The world's abundance-economic systems therefore require immediate change. We face a system break—a change from one system, in which a particular set of understandings and rules worked effectively, to a fundamentally new system, which requires new understandings and policies. Mankind has already undergone two such system breaks in the past—one from hunting and gathering to agriculture, and the other from agriculture to industry. The present, third system break is from industry to cybernation: the combination of men with machine systems. Controlling and benefiting from cybernation will be possible only if we learn to communicate more honestly and efficiently than we do today.

The successful management of system breaks requires that people successfully develop new perceptions of the way in which the universe is ordered. As new perceptions develop, people discover new views about their self-interest. These new views then control their future actions. Out of these new understandings and new patterns of self-interest emerge changed policies.

The key economic reality to which our thinking is geared is scarcity: we believe that there is not enough of anything to go round. Our lives are ordered by a pursuit of material goals, because we are afraid that not enough can be produced to satisfy our needs, which we assume are insatiable. We have not understood that abundance is feasible and could already exist if only we would reorganize our socioeconomic systems.

Why are we so afraid of abundance, and why is there so much support for the continuation of an economics built on scarcity assumptions? The most recent basis is the fear that perception of the reality of abundance will lead people to be careless of economic resources. This, however, misunderstands the reasons behind the present drive for material goods and the psychological changes that will occur when we recognize the existence of a state of abundance.

Acceptance of the reality of abundance would destroy our present insecurities, which drive us to conspicuous consumption. Once we know that we are capable of producing enough, there will be no practical, or psychological, possibility of demonstrating power or superiority by consuming more goods and services. Man, who constantly seeks new challenges, will reorient his life and find new sources of satisfaction in his own creative self-development. He will openly express himself instead of demonstrating through goods the façade he wishes other people to see.

At the present time, only the postindustrial countries possess the abundance on which psychological, cultural, and socioeconomic reorientation could be based. Early industrial and preindustrial countries will continue to be limited by scarcity for some time to come—how long a time depends to a large extent on how quickly the abundance-regions recognize the reality of their own abundance. Once the existence of adequate resources is internalized as part of the abundance-region thought patterns, consumer societies will become creative societies. This will liberate not only goods and resources but also creativity, which can be employed in a world-wide effort to eliminate scarcity. (This book will exclude the problems of the scarcity regions except in the epilogue.)

The main socioeconomic reinforcement for scarcity economics is the measuring systems that we have created to evaluate "success" and "failure." We measure success by the rate of growth in Gross National Product, failure by high unemployment rates. In abundance regions it is still essentially assumed, despite all the evidence to the contrary, that if a high rate of growth is being attained, improvement in educational, social, and ethical patterns will occur. While support for this view has admittedly diminished following the social developments which have accompanied the economic boom of the sixties, we have not yet abandoned this belief.

John Cage, the artist, has stated that "Measurements measure measuring means." In other words, what and how we measure explains more about our culture than statistical changes in the measurements. We measure economic growth because we have been convinced that it is *the* important reality. It is only recently that we have begun to search for new measurements which will enable us to discover the implications of changes in our social relations, in our educational skills, and in our ethics. We are now learning that improvements in these patterns do not necessarily occur if there is economic growth. Indeed, we have increasingly clear evidence that economic growth may be negatively correlated with societal, educational, and ethical changes.

This argument, however, takes us beyond the limits of this book. We are interested here in describing the process by which scarcity economics has come to dominate our thought patterns, the changes in economic theory and practice which are necessary, and the ways in which these changes can be achieved. This book argues that our incorrect economic theories and practice are one of the major factors preventing us from intelligent policy making in all fields.

Any split between the economic aspects of life and the remainder of man's activities is, of course, unrealistic: all issues are interconnected. However, we have isolated economics from our other activities for so long that our present incorrect economic policies must be directly and specifically challenged if significant changes are to occur.

It is now argued, with increasing frequency, that economics has become an obsolete science, that policies for the emerging era cannot be formulated with the industrial-era tool of economics, that economics is adapted only to scarcity conditions. Instead of challenging economists to extend their theory to cover the new realities, this kind of criticism states flatly that economics has become inapplicable, and implicitly assumes that economic thinking will simply "go away" because it has been dismissed as irrelevant.

This view ignores the existing reality of economic dominance of our present thought patterns. A time will come when we are so accustomed to a state of abundance that we are unaware of its existence; but in order to reach that time we must become highly aware of abundance now. This can only be done if we develop out of economics into socioeconomics. Scarcity-economic thinking has not automatically diminished in the face of negating reality and will not do so; it must be shown that a serious consideration of what we already know in economics will force us to move on to socioeconomics.

An effective transition from economic to socioeconomic thinking will necessarily be gradual; this book discusses only the first steps. The body of the text describes what we are moving away from—scarcity economics within a context of abundance—and also sketches how the move can be made. The epilogue begins to examine where we are heading: toward socioeconomics in a context of world-wide abundance.

We must always remember that the history of the past two hundred years has been largely dominated by our changing economic philosophy. Adam Smith, Malthus, Ricardo, Marx, Schumpeter, and Keynes have all altered our view of the way in which the world is put together, and as a result have changed the thinking of our self-interest and our patterns of action. As Keynes himself put it, "Soon or late, it is ideas and not men which rule the world."

The extraordinary power which our society has accorded to economists is based in large part on the fact that the public usually believes that economists serve as technicians, that they make decisions about how best to achieve goals which have been predetermined by the society. In reality, however, they have always acted to set the goals for the society. We have now reached the point where scarcity economists must be challenged to describe and justify the political, social, and ethical implications of their theories and policies. As a corollary, the public must recognize that a viable socioeconomy depends on the extent to which individuals accept the responsibility for making most of their own socioeconomic decisions rather than relying on bureaucratic government.

The aim of this book is to stimulate both these developments: to help the noneconomist to understand the nature and implications of economic decisions, and to discuss the process of expanding economics into socioeconomics. Economic jargon will therefore be kept to a minimum. It is assumed that economists will recognize familiar arguments in nonjargon terms.

In conclusion, I should note that the nature of the book dictates its content. This book discusses a fundamentally new concept of the necessary way to reorder the economic system. It would therefore be premature to make developed, detailed proposals which would detract from a concentration on the *basic* assumptions and arguments.

If the assumptions and arguments of this book prove to be relevant, we will need to rethink all existing economic policies and to study how necessary new policies can be introduced. It is my hope that those who read this volume—particularly those in colleges and universities—will particpate in the challenge of this development. Freed from the deadweight of past incorrect expertise, they can create new knowledge directly relevant to the conditions observable around them.

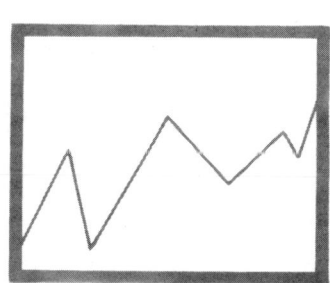

ECONOMIC THEORY— PAST, PRESENT, AND FUTURE

A BRIEF
HISTORY
OF RECENT
ECONOMIC
THOUGHT

During the decade of the sixties, the United States grew richer at a very rapid rate. Or so the available statistics tell us! Why then do so many feel poorer as we enter the seventies?

Some people are poorer. The incomes of many of the old, the disabled, and others, have not kept up with the rate of inflation. Similarly, the wages of many workers have risen too slowly to compensate for the effect of rising prices.

But even those who have more money and therefore can buy more than in the past often *feel* worse off. They find that even if they have more money they are able to buy fewer of the things they want. For example, they are forced to spend large sums to protect themselves from robbery and violence and from the effects of environmental pollution. In addition, when their small appliances, such as radios and coffee percolaters, break down, they are all too often confronted with highly inadequate repair services charging excessive fees, and the individual must choose between paying large sums for often inefficient service or scrapping the product and repurchasing. In a very real sense, money doesn't buy what it used to. The costs of the breakdown in the quality of life are directly reflected in each individual's budget.

Why is this happening? The discipline of economics *should* help people to understand the economic forces which confront them. Unfortunately, at the present time it does not. The primary reason for this situation is that economists are operating with out-of-date assumptions which do not reflect today's real world. In addition, economists often choose to present their conclusions in language which prevents the layman from understanding what is really happening in the economic system.

This book aims to explain the real forces which determine our incomes, our expenditures, rates of economic growth, and rates of inflation. While there is no short cut to understanding these issues, the committed reader will have no difficulty in following the argument. The conventional jargon of economists has been carefully avoided.

The discipline of economics is concerned with two levels of theory. First, it aims to discover the general relationships between production, consumption, saving, and population, as well as the ways in which these can be manipulated to achieve economic growth. This study of the *total* economy is called *macroeconomics*. Macroeconomics is concerned with the size of a nation's economic pie (the Gross National Product), how fast it increases from year to year, and how many people share it.

Second, the discipline of economics is interested in the detailed relationships between the prices of various goods and services, the relative wages and salaries paid for various types of activities, the determinants of the rate of interest, and so on. This study of the various parts of the socioeconomy is called *microeconomics*. Microeconomics is concerned with the distribution of the economic pie, who gets what share of total production, and how the pie is produced.

Macroeconomic and microeconomic theories and analysis emerged at different times and from different sources out of what used to be called "political economy." This chapter will trace briefly the historical roots of macroeconomics and microeconomics, and examine whether the two levels of economics can be reconciled. *We shall discover that not only are the assumptions behind macroeconomics and microeconomics contradictory but also that neither of them provides a realistic basis for policy in present conditions.*

Adam Smith, whose major work, *The Wealth of Nations*, was published in England about two hundred years ago, is generally considered to be the father of modern economics: both macroeconomic issues and microeconomic issues were examined by him.

Smith's long-run achievements were in three primary directions. First, he showed that in the industrial era the ability to increase production depended upon the degree of specialization—or, as he described it, "the division of labor." This insight contributed to the creation of the assembly line late in the nineteenth and early in the twentieth centuries.

Second, he showed that the degree of specialization in the industrial era was limited by the extent of the market—the number of people to whom the goods produced might be sold. He therefore argued that measures should be taken to minimize external and internal barriers to trade in order to increase potential sales. For external trade, this argument became formalized as the doctrine of free trade, which stated that there should be no barriers to imports or exports.

The third influence of Adam Smith's work would surprise and probably disturb him. His work actually served to move the economics profession away from the macroeconomic issues in which Smith was primarily interested toward microeconomics. In his book, Smith continued the understanding which had long been basic to economics, that market forces, which came to be called the "invisible hand," somehow insured a rough equivalence between value and price. However, Smith failed to understand why goods which were valuable *in use* (such as water and air) were often less valuable *in exchange* than goods (such as diamonds) which have little value in use. This issue, which was unresolved by Smith, came to absorb more and more of the attention of economists over the next hundred years.

The question was finally solved in the 1870s by a school of economists which came to be called the neoclassicists. Once solved, the answer became obvious. The neoclassicists showed that price depends on both supply and demand. Goods which are essential will be cheap—or even free—if they are abundant enough. Goods which are nonessential, or luxuries, will be expensive if part, or all, of the population has more than enough money to satisfy its needs for essentials and also desires nonessentials to indicate status or demand prestige.

This argument is one of the basic—and correct—theses of economics today. However, the neoclassicists' work went much further. They developed a theory which argued that market forces operating by themselves would insure maximum efficiency of production and also insure that each person received the value of his production. It is now possible to state clearly the assumptions which must be fulfilled if the neoclassical theory is to be valid:

1. Human beings must be "economic men" ruled entirely by economic motivations. They must not consider social or psychological satisfactions.
2. All firms must be small—in other words, no firm should be able to use power to distort the market for its own advantage.
3. There must be no labor unions—workers must not be able to combine to attain power to raise wages.
4. There must be no government intervention in the economy—the power of government must not be used to alter prices of goods and services or to distort wages and salaries.

5. There must be correct information available so that people can move into those activities which will be most profitable to them.
6. There must be no fundamental changes in conditions—economic, technical, social, etc.—over time. The neoclassical thesis is valid only for static and not for dynamic conditions.

The implications of this set of assumptions became a will-o'-the-wisp for succeeding generations of economists. *If* neoclassical assumptions were accepted as true, economics became a "pure" science. Economists appeared to have effectively eliminated from their discipline the complexity of man as well as the economic, social, and political issues raised by power. The elimination of complexity and power created a theoretical world in which it was possible to draw firm conclusions and to develop increasingly detailed theories.

The willingness to move so far away from the real world seems extraordinary today. We must remember, however, that changes in economic thinking formed part of a massive nineteenth-century trend. During this century, the drive to abandon the study of complex reality and to create simplified theoretical models was dominant. In addition, the second half of the nineteenth century was a period in which it was believed that mechanical analogies were adequate to explain all realities.

The direction of economics therefore received support from all sides, for it seemed to many as though economics had made the first breakthrough into a machine-like social science. It was rather generally assumed that highly significant practical results would follow once the full implications of "mechanical" economics had been developed, and that these results would be generalizable to the other social sciences.

The costs of this development can now be seen, but only with the aid of hindsight. Because economists were not themselves clear about the fact that they had actually abandoned the study of reality, they failed to appreciate to the full the potential contributions to the discipline of economists such as Schumpeter, Pigou, and the members of the institutional school. In effect, the economics profession has lived since the time of the neoclassicists in a world well described by Albert Lauterbach in a 1950 article: ". . . Economic theory has faced from its beginning two basic alternatives in its assumptions on human behavior. It could either operate with the known motivations of human beings in the real world in so far as they affect the market and other material processes in society; or it could proceed on the basis of hypothetical assumptions concerning human attitudes and reactions, and work out functional relations which would be valid only if and when people behaved in this hypothetical way (which was then classified as economic). By and large, the second attitude prevailed, although this often occurred in confused or unconscious combination with the first. It was as if a physicist, before calculating the velocity of fall under actual conditions of a given air density, altitude etc. had calculated the velocity in a vacuum without keeping out all the complicating factors at first and without introducing all of them eventually either. . . ."

Failure to perceive the need for more realistic assumptions and new possible directions for the discipline was, however, only part of the problem. Economists were so committed to the neoclassical theoretical model that they directed their policy actions to insuring that the real world conformed as closely as possible to the model whose implications they were studying. They tried during sixty years to promote those developments which would cause the real world to move toward their neoclassical assumptions and to limit those which caused the real world to diverge from them. Thus they attempted to infuse the culture with "economic" thinking, to limit the size of firms, to prevent the development of unions, and to decrease government intervention. They were, however, little concerned with promoting accuracy of information movement, for its critical importance in validating their model was not yet really understood.

The consequent pattern of economic policy was highly unsatisfactory, for two reasons. First, neoclassical theory never did prove that a free-market system was best, or more just, for the society as a whole; it only proved that under certain circumstances it caused maximum efficiency in the economy. During this period, economists were therefore equating, without any real proof, the efficiency of the economy with the welfare of the society and the development of the culture. The dangers in this attitude are now increasingly clear.

Second, the power of economists to prevent developments which destroyed the validity of their assumptions varied with the groups they were attempting to control. Economists in America were largely successful in holding back the growth of unions till the thirties. They were reasonably successful in preventing the growth of government action. They had little success in stopping the massive expansion of large corporations: during this period corporations grew so rapidly that they came to dominate the operation of the economy. *The prime effect, therefore, of economic manipulation between 1875 and 1930 was to promote the interests of corporations as against those of the unions and those of the total society as represented by the government.* The fact that this increase in the relative power of corporations was unintended did not make it any less real.

This reality became so obvious and the microeconomic theory of the neoclassicists became so clearly unsatisfactory that it was challenged simultaneously by young economists in England and the United States. These analysts demonstrated that when the six neoclassical assumptions were *not* met, those "marketives" which had the ability to use power would obtain a higher percentage of national resources than would have been theirs under free market conditions. *They showed, in other words, that power could be directly translated into changes in the distribution of resources.* (The word *marketive,* meaning all those who sell goods and services—individuals, firms, corporations, conglomerates, etc.—

will be used from this point onward in the book where a collective noun is needed to cover all sellers of goods and services. The word *marketive* was first introduced in 1962.)

It can now be stated that in the industrial era, *economics is a branch of politics.* Those who have been given or have seized most power will obtain the largest share of the resources produced by their society. They will achieve this result by limiting supply and by encouraging demand: both of these activities will raise the price they can obtain for the "ecofacts" they sell. (The word *ecofact,* meaning any good or service exchanged for money — minerals, agricultural products, durable goods, nondurable goods, services, etc. — will be used from this point onward in the book where a collective noun is needed to cover all goods and services that are sold. The word *ecofact* was first introduced in 1962. In the epilogue ecofacts will be contrasted with sociofacts — goods and services whose exchange is mediated by factors other than money.)

The discipline of economics is schismatic about microeconomics today. On the one hand, no competent economist would suggest that neoclassical microeconomic theory is valid: no one is prepared to argue that the actual distribution of economic resources reflects the real contribution of people to the economic system or that it insures maximum effectiveness in production. On the other hand, economists continue to make policy *as though* microeconomics were valid. This reality is clear, for example, in the failure of economists to come to grips with the implications of the fact that agriculturalists have less power than industrialists, that those who earn low wages almost always have less power than those earning higher wages.

Economists have been able to persist in this schismatic attitude for the forty years since microeconomic theory was effectively challenged, because neither the discipline of economics nor the society has been particularly interested during these years in the factors which determine the *distribution* of the available economic pie. We have been almost exclusively concerned with the macroeconomic factors which determine the size of the economic pie and its rate of growth.

The failure to follow through on our new understanding of the reality determining the distribution of income has had two profound consequences. First, it has dangerously delayed the necessary reexamination of the factors which *should* shape the distribution of resources, as opposed to those which do presently shape them. In effect, we have continued to act as though present patterns were both just and desirable. Second, we have continued to assume that we have effective ways to understand and measure the operation of the economic system through studying indices of production, income, Gross National Product, etc.

In fact, all our monetary systems of measurement are incorrect because of the distortions in value produced by the use of power. We must face up to the fact that *in present circumstances* there are *no* accurate measures of economic value; this means that we possess no really meaningful statistics to permit us to evaluate the operation of the economy.

The prime requirement for a good measuring tool is that it remains constant. Our existing systems of measurement change all the time. As we are not aware of the extent—indeed not even always of the direction—of change, our interpretation of economic statistics is inaccurate at best and dangerously misleading at worst.

The patterns of economic analysis of the last thirty years are the consequence of the development of the major macroeconomic crisis of the thirties. This crisis was not inevitable; it was caused in large part by faulty economic theory. We have seen that neoclassical theory "proved," on the basis of six primary assumptions, that the economy would operate with maximum effectiveness in the absence of intervention. Neoclassicists assumed that the rate of interest would act in such a way as to insure that not only would each resource needed in the economy be employed as usefully as possible, but also that *all* resources with any economic value would inevitably find employment. Despite the frequency of slumps, economists had been blinded to their real significance, for they had not developed any theory to explain them. It was not until the massive crisis of the thirties that economists came to concentrate on this problem. As the economics profession moved in this direction it became increasingly uninterested in the problems emerging from distortions in the distribution of income.

The change in the focus of interest of economists has been largely credited to John Maynard Keynes's book *The General Theory of Employment, Interest and Money*. In this book, Keynes showed that there was *no automatic* mechanism that would insure that production and consumption remained in balance. He proved that government intervention was essential to avoid slumps.

Keynes's work, however, was far more limited in its implications than has so far been understood. As in the case of the neoclassicists, Keynesian analysis applies only if certain restrictive assumptions are fulfilled. Keynes stated them in the following way: "We take as given the existing skill and quantity of available labor, the existing quantity and quality of available equipment, the existing technique. This does not mean that we assume these facts to be constant but merely that in this place and context, we are not considering or taking into account the effects and consequences of changes in them." In other words, Keynes ignored for the purpose of his book the most dynamic elements in a late industrial-era economy.

The economics profession adopted the same pattern after the development of Keynesian theory as it did with neoclassical theory. Instead of primarily studying the results of removing the restrictive conditions originally used by Keynes, economists have spent their time developing further theories about *how the world would behave if Keynes's assumptions were valid*. They acted in this way despite an explicit warning by Keynes of the need for new views of the economic system and despite the obvious reality that the restrictive assumptions imposed by Keynes obviously were becoming less and less accurate. Keynes argued: "... when the accumulation of wealth is no longer of high social importance, there will be great changes in the code of morals. We shall be able to rid ourselves of many of the pseudo-moral principles which have hag-ridden us for two hundred years, by which we have exalted some of the most distasteful of human qualities into the position of the highest values. We shall be able to afford to dare to assess the money-motive at its true value .... All kinds of social customs and economic practices affecting the distribution of wealth and its rewards and penalties which we now maintain at all costs, however distasteful and unjust they may be in themselves ... we shall then be free, at last, to discard."

The development of Keynesian theory into neo-Keynesian theory and practice has dominated the discipline of economics for the last generation. The process of introducing neo-Keynesian policies was completed most rapidly in England. By the end of the Second World War, it was accepted there that the government should play an active role in maximizing production, maximizing growth, and minimizing unemployment. By the beginning of the sixties, all the Western industrial-era countries were taking active steps to attempt to achieve these ends. The United States was the last of these countries to accept fully the neo-Keynesian prescription, but the economic stagnation of the fifties finally led to full recognition of the dangers of government passivity in a late industrial-era system: there had been half-hearted attempts both in the thirties and in post-war years but full commitment waited till the sixties.

The economic *successes* of the first half of the sixties resulted from Presidents Kennedy and Johnson applying neo-Keynesian policies. The economic *failures* of the second half of the sixties stem from the limitations of neo-Keynesianism. Given the present pace of technological change, it is impossible to reach meaningful conclusions if one excludes from one's concerns, as Keynes did, "the existing skill and quantity of available labor, the existing quality and quantity of available equipment, the existing technique." All of these factors, and primarily the last of them, are dominant creators of trends in today's economy.

It is important to note, once again, that economists would certainly deny that they exclude the relevant factors of analysis. But, as Lauterbach stated in the quotation cited earlier in this chapter, the realities of technological change have not been built into the basic model but are only additions to it.

A model can be valid only if it includes all the critical elements in the real world it is meant to depict, for otherwise the conclusions derived from the model must necessarily be incorrect. In effect, Keynesian assumptions actually exclude *all* the factors most critical in determining levels and types of unemployment in a cybernetic era. The growth of information is now so rapid that many people are ceasing to be able to compete with machine systems incorporating this new information—they are becoming unemployable at any wage. This reality, and any realistic study of the ways to deal with it, are "excluded" by the Keynesian set of assumptions.

The obsolescence of Keynesian theory has been further hastened by the additional assumptions introduced by the neo-Keynesians. These additional assumptions, which are seldom made explicit, can be stated as follows:

1. Wants are unlimited. This article of faith is always affirmed and never proved.
2. Work will be effectively performed only if it is structured into jobs and economic incentives are so patterned that people are forced to hold jobs.
3. The costs of economic growth, in terms of environmental degradation affecting both the individual and the society, can be ignored.

Some of the consequences that follow from this set of assumptions are *not* immediately obvious. Economists are forced to act to maintain certain patterns of behavior if the validity of neo-Keynesian theory is to continue. In particular, they must ensure that almost all those who desire a job are able to find one. This, in turn, has two major consequences:

1. It is essential that the public be prepared to purchase all the ecofacts which can be produced; if such a willingness is not insured, there will obviously be a shortage of jobs. This means, in turn, that economists must be prepared to accept—and usually encourage—any activity which increases pressures toward consumption, regardless of their effect on the quality of life.
2. Because very few people can obtain a decent standard of living without holding a job, economists must find ways to insure that every family unit has at least one breadwinner in it. This means, of course, that those who are displaced by technology must be constantly retrained: as a consequence, the individual is all too often seen as a faulty machine rather than as a human being.

Given these realities, the implications of neo-Keynesian policies can be clearly stated. It is the responsibility of the government to balance the economy to insure maximum economic growth: this will satisfy people's growing wants. Jobs must be available for all so that the necessary work will be done and so that incomes can be provided through job holding. Costs of these processes can be ignored as insignificant.

This neo-Keynesian policy statement is becoming unacceptable to the public. Three factors are bringing about this result: one of them is already easily recognizable, the second is still largely hidden, and the third is only just emerging.

First, it is now clear that a large segment of the American people is deciding that a healthy, livable environment is at least as important to them as further economic growth. As present patterns of economic growth do create massive pollution of the environment, this change in priorities means that there will be growing pressure to limit economic growth in the future. Ecological concerns will mobilize significant parts of public opinion against economic growth for the first time in American history: some ecological groups are already calling for a "no-growth economy." (We shall see in the last chapter, entitled "Short-Run Economic Issues," that this reaction is dangerous. It seems certain, nevertheless, that it will be strongly supported.)

The signs of the change in attitude toward the environment are everywhere. It is almost impossible to pick up a magazine without reading about the environmental and ecological crisis. Cities and communities across America and Europe are forming groups to preserve, or re-create, the purity of their own air and water. As we enter the seventies, the American government is clearly trying to capture the political benefits believed to be available from the issue.

Second, people are finding that as their income increases they wish to spend less time in earning money, purchasing ecofacts, and maintaining them. Instead, they want to find time to enjoy what they already possess. This result could have been anticipated on the basis of existing economic theory. It has been agreed for at least a century that people tend to balance additional units of satisfaction from different ways of using resources. It follows that as people earn more money, they will tend to work less, for they will be able to satisfy more of their consumption needs with the same time at work. This trend has been prevented from emerging up to the present time only by the pressure which existed for individuals to increase their tastes. Until the sixties, the consumption ethic was very strong and only a few people resisted the pressure to go on buying regardless of real need. During the sixties, a growing number of people—largely among the young— decided that consumption was valuable only as a means to an end and not as an end in itself. As we enter the seventies, a movement to limit consumption is growing rapidly.

Third, a crisis is developing in terms of labor policies. During the thirties, the labor unions in America gained significant power. Strong societal support had developed for the concept of workers' rights, largely in reaction to the excessive power which marketives had gained as a result of the actions of neoclassical economists. Since World War II, a commitment has also developed that everybody should be able to find a job. Unfortunately, it is now becoming clear that the inadequate education given to many when they were young unfits them for the tasks which will be available after machine systems develop their potentials.

Our immediate economic crisis, which makes it impossible to combine low levels of unemployment with price stability in a growth economy, thus joins with a profound conceptual crisis. The economic assumptions within which we presently reason are so inadequate to describe the real world that they provide us with no basis for developing intelligent policies.

As a result, the economic dilemma of all late-industrial-era countries is far deeper than has so far been realized. The policies needed to end the slump of the 1930s were in fact known by the mid-thirties, but they could not be applied because they were socially and politically unacceptable. The policies needed to solve the present economic dilemma are now growing clear, but, as we shall see, they are not socially or politically acceptable at this time.

The minimum requirement, therefore, if we are to achieve a successful economic policy in the seventies is to educate people to the fact that the economic system within which they are living is no longer functional and that it must be replaced. Experience shows that this task will be profoundly difficult, because changes in the economic system directly affect the self-interest of the individual.

In reality, we are confronted with two tasks, only one of which will be examined in this volume. First, we must create new economic theory. Second, we must develop ways to permit people to discover that this new economic theory and the policies which stem from it are necessary to the creation of a better society—and indeed to our survival.

A NEW THEORETICAL UNDERSTANDING

During every discussion of economic theory a large sign should be displayed: "Always Test Your Assumptions Against Real Conditions."

Had this essential reminder continuously formed part of economic thinking during the past hundred years, much of the theoretical slippage would have been avoided, and today's society would not be confronted with ugliness and confusion on all sides. However, just as nineteenth-century architects covered contemporary iron-skeleton construction with a jumble of gothic, renaissance, classical, and romanesque exteriors, so nineteenth-century economists covered the implications of the economic developments of their time by invalid theory. When microeconomics ceased to be valid, they would turn their attention to macroeconomic patterns. And so, shuttling between the two levels of economic analysis, manipulating a jumble of models, assumptions, theories, facts, and statistics, economics advanced loftily throughout the twentieth century never caring about the consequent complete confusion of the layman.

We must come to terms with the current reality. The theory and practice of economics are in disarray.

We can see this most clearly if we start this chapter by summarizing what has already been stated and then drawing the primary conclusion. We no longer possess a satisfactory theoretical explanation of either microeconomics or macroeconomics. In microeconomics, it is known that power rather than market forces is the prime determinant of prices, wages, and salaries, but economists have not taken the time to discover the new systematic theory of income distribution which is inherent in this reality. In macroeconomics, while there is no general agreement on the exact nature of the theoretical breakdown, it is clear that neo-Keynesian theories are no longer adequate.

Theoretical failures are complicated by several immediate policy crises. First, it is clear that full employment and reasonable levels of price stability are not compatible. If we continue today's patterns of thinking, we will necessarily suffer either from increasing inflation or from increasing unemployment or both.

Second, there is a growing fundamental challenge to existing patterns of income distribution. This takes two major forms. There is the demand of the poor for a larger share of resources which would provide them with adequate incomes. There is the demand of the middle class that they should pay no more than their fair share of taxes. In addition, of course, those who are rich because of their privileged power position are always alert to prevent its erosion.

Third, there is a growing understanding of a need for a change in economic attitudes toward raw materials, land, and all natural resources. Up to this point, the environmental effects of economic policies have been largely ignored; today, citizens are demanding that they be given prime consideration. The public is coming to require not only the ending of pollution but also the creation of a desirable environment, in which the benefits of personal abundance can be effectively realized.

Given these theoretical and practical issues, the attitude of the practitioners of the profession of economics today is not only largely irrelevant but also profoundly dangerous. In fact, there is still a basic tendency in the profession to act as though there were no real theoretical contradictions and no possibility of a serious economic crisis. If this attitude should persist for an extended period of years, the already-declining influence of economists will be destroyed. In addition, the consequent delay in dealing with many urgent issues would insure further development of present trends and make it even more difficult to act creatively.

A NEW CYBERNETIC APPROACH TO THE SOCIAL SCIENCES

The situation we presently confront is exceptionally difficult. Indeed, our problems might well be insoluble if we did not already possess the intellectual tools required to handle them. (The development of fundamentally new concepts is always time consuming, and the period required is always unpredictable.) Fortunately, however, we can apply to economic theory and practice the knowledge already gained by cybernetics—knowledge concerned with the science of communication.

The cyberneticist analyzes everything as a system; systems are always part of larger systems and contain smaller systems. A ship with all her passengers, crew, and equipment is a system. It is part of the larger system which contains all the ships owned and operated by the company; a ship contains many subsystems, ranging from the methods of providing food to that of steering.

A redwood forest is a system. It is part of the larger system in which the survival of the redwood forest is based on conflicting human priorities; it contains many subsystems, ranging from each individual tree to the relationships between the trees and the other life within the forest. One of the key necessities for effective cybernetic thinking, therefore, is to determine the relevant system to be studied and acted upon and to draw appropriate boundaries around it.

Cyberneticists are interested in all systems, whatever their length of life. People may come together in a system to help an accident victim; such a group is temporary. A system may be formed to carry out a particular task, and may disband when the goal is reached. Systems may be long-lived, such as a university or a nation. Each type of system is organized differently; the time that a group hopes to survive has profound implications for the form it adopts.

Cyberneticists emphasize that groups are never single-goaled. In particular, in the context of this book, we must recognize that economic organizations—labor unions, the National Chamber of Commerce, marketives, and so on—are made up of human beings with concerns and priorities which mesh only partially with the goals at their places of employment. Thus, although the apparent primary goal of a marketive is to sell ecofacts at a profit, each individual within it will have his own motivations. Some of these, such as personal ambition, will tend to reinforce the stated goal of the marketive; others, such as love of family or religious concerns, may cut across it.

The science of cybernetics is based on a simple core statement. Any social, or other, system must be able to adapt to changing circumstances if it is to survive. There are two critical steps in this continuing process; one can start examining the process from either point:

1. There must be the possibility for effective decision making. This requires that some parts of the system take the responsi-

bility for decisions about the situation as it confronts them. The more flexible the system, the more the decision about responsibility for action will necessarily be based on self-perception and self-motivation.

We can contrast the system involved in the "decision" of a tree to grow its leaves in the spring with the decision of the society to do something about pollution. In the case of the tree, an automatic mechanism is triggered by the warmer weather or some other change in the seasonal pattern. (If the weather is prematurely hot early in the year, the tree may "decide" wrongly.) In the case of pollution, some individuals must decide that it is *their* responsibility to alert the society to the dangers of pollution. Until they begin to do so, they cannot be certain that the task is essential or that the channels exist to make possible effective communication.

2. Decisions always entail consequences. *Even if* the decision made is ideal and provides a maximum favorable response (a situation seldom realized in complex human systems), the decision will necessarily change the initial situation, and further action will inevitably be required.

In the more probable case, the decision will have been less than ideal, and there will be a necessity for correction of the original decision. In either case, *accurate* feedback will be required to permit evaluation of the new situation brought into existence by the decision.

The channels for feedback may be fixed, as in the case of a tree, or they may be open and uncertain, as when people are trying to draw the attention of the society to the issue of pollution. Those engaging in drawing the attention of the society to new issues will have to evaluate highly contradictory feedback patterns if they are to determine the effectiveness of their previous action. It must be particularly noted that in today's conditions the problems of decision makers in evaluating feedback are made even more complicated because of its deliberate distortion.

Once the feedback has been evaluated, new decisions can be made. It becomes obvious, following the discussion of feedback above, that the relevance of the decision depends on the accuracy of the feedback, on correct evaluation of the feedback, and a willingness to act upon it. The feedback–decision–feedback–decision–feedback etc. process is a necessity for any system if it is to continue to exist.

We can now state two further implications of this analysis. A system must so manage its relationships with the larger systems of which it is a part that it is permitted or encouraged to continue in existence. It must so manage its relationships with the smaller systems which comprise it that they continue to act in the ways necessary for its continued existence. Secondly, those evaluating feedback must have the knowledge required to draw correct conclusions.

DECISION MAKING AND FEEDBACK

The classic textbook illustration of a cybernetic decision-making circuit is the thermostat; this will provide us with a good starting point for our discussion. We shall discover, later, that the analogy between a thermostat and a social system must not be pushed too far, for it becomes misleading and prevents us from perceiving some of the most critical issues involved in communication.

A thermostat—we shall use throughout this chapter the example of a thermostat which is designed to heat a room—is an adjustable mechanism which insures that the temperature remains at a desired level. It consists of a temperature-sensing device that signals a heating mechanism when to turn itself on and off.

Economists have understood since the time of the Greeks that "market forces" serve such a thermostatic function in economic affairs. For example, if people demand more of an ecofact than before, the price will tend to rise and the profit to be made by selling it will also rise. This rise in price will make it attractive for more people to produce and sell the particular ecofact, thus bringing the price down again. If, on the other hand, people demand less of an ecofact than before, the price will tend to fall, as will profits. This will drive people out of the business of producing and selling the particular ecofact, and the consequent reduction in supply will increase the price again.

UNINTENDED DISTORTIONS OF DECISION MAKING AND FEEDBACK

What forces operate to prevent decision making and feedback from being effective? We shall use the thermostat analogy to illustrate the less complex cases.

One possible problem with the operation of a thermostat is that it may get out of phase, or "hunt." This pattern occurs when the thermostat is insensitive, oversensitive, or badly placed, and thus reacts too slowly or rapidly to changes in the temperature. In these circumstances, the signals to the heating mechanism are made at the wrong time. In effect, the furnace is turned off when it should be turned on and vice versa. The feedback is inappropriate, and the thermostat makes its "decision" on the basis of incorrect data.

The equivalent problem has long been studied in economics: the classic case is known as the "hog cycle." The hog cycle occurs because hog producers tend to react to the price as it is at the time of breeding rather than the price which will exist at the time the hogs reach the market. Thus producers breed most pigs when market prices are high. This leads to peak marketing of hogs several months later, and prices therefore fall. Producers of hogs then become depressed about market prospects and cut back on their breeding. Several months later, therefore, the quantity of pigs available for marketing is reduced and prices rise. This causes the cycle to start again. It has been shown that the cycle tends to perpetuate itself because of the time it takes to get pigs to market after breeding; another time period would have led to automatic damping of the cycle.

When one has identified the problem of "hunting" in a thermostat or in a particular part of the economic system as the source of inefficient decision making, more appropriate placing of feedback mechanisms or increased knowledge of how to interpret the feedback signals will reduce or eliminate the problem.

Two other unintended causes of poor feedback and decision making can be identified. They are analogous to the situation in which a thermostat exists but is not connected up to the furnace, and to that in which a thermostat has been wrongly connected so that an attempt to reduce the temperature actually raises it, and vice versa.

In the first case, incorrect information may exist about the operation of the economic system. This may lead to the belief that there is a connection between two parts of the economic system when there is actually no significant connection. One may therefore attempt to change one part of the economic system by altering another only to find that nothing happens. Or, more probably, it may actually be impossible to determine if something has happened because of the many factors impinging on the two aspects thought to be connected.

In the second case, which is usually more serious, it is believed that one economic factor relates to another in one way when the relationship is actually the direct opposite. For example, the policies which were employed by the Nixon Administration in 1969 were based on the argument that inflation can be reduced by tight money, high interest rates, and low rates of economic growth. It can be argued that these policies have little effect in an economy where everybody believes in the continuation of neo-Keynesian growth policies. It is even possible that the policies employed in 1969 actually increased inflation.

DELIBERATE DISTORTIONS OF DECISION MAKING AND FEEDBACK

It can be assumed that those who rely on a thermostat are interested that its feedback should be accurate and uninterrupted. This is not true in the case of an economic system: it is often in the interest of individuals to distort information deliberately or to prevent free access to accurate information. This section of the book will deal with the ways in which privileged access to accurate information can be used to increase control over resources. One simple example may be useful as a starting point. It is now well known that those who buy and sell stocks and who can afford to employ people with immediate access to the most accurate information will be more successful than the small investor who does not have such access.

Distortion of information can be designed for short-run purposes. We can see how this works by looking at the thermostat again. Let us suppose that somebody holds a match next to the sensing mechanism of the thermostat; in these conditions, the thermostat will be tricked into "believing" that the room is hotter than it is, and will cease to heat it. The effect, of course, will be temporary, and will reverse itself after the match is withdrawn.

Attempts are often made to engage in such short-run trickery of the economic system. Because prices tend to fall when demand is low or supply is high, marketives endeavor to conceal any slump in demand or excess in supply which weakens their position to demand a high price. Bluff is often used in economic bargaining to force better terms than would have been available if real conditions had been known.

There has been decreasing emphasis, however, on attempts to achieve short-run distortions. It is increasingly understood that feedback mechanisms will often operate rapidly to eliminate short-run gains. The major search today is to discover longer-run methods of tricking the economic system; methods are sought which permit marketives to continue to distort information so as to create artificial scarcity and insure high prices without being interrupted by corrective feedback.

The parallel in the case of a thermostat would be to surround it permanently with ice. In these circumstances, the heat would operate consistently and the temperature would rise until the limit of the heating capacity of the furnace was reached.

In one profound sense, the economic history of the twentieth century can be described in terms of an increasing attempt to discover how to trick the economic mechanism permanently. This has involved finding new techniques of distortion, and has also required control of feedback channels to prevent the distortion from being corrected by feedback. It would be impossible to describe, or even list, all the methods used for this purpose, but they break down into two main categories: those affecting demand and those affecting supply.

Demand

Marketives aim to increase the demand for their ecofacts, for this tends to increase the price that can be charged.

Each individual's perception of the satisfaction available from the ecofacts he chooses to purchase is primarily subjective. There is, of course, an objective core because people need certain levels of food, clothing, and shelter to survive. But it is certainly obvious that the expenditures required for mere survival would only take a minor proportion of the available average income in abundance areas.

The primary factor which affects subjective perceptions of ecofacts is that each culture and subculture places a higher value on certain types of ecofacts than on others. These patterns of cultural evaluation of ecofacts limit and control to a greater or lesser extent the behavior of every individual within the society or culture.

Marketives today, therefore, aim to find ways to induce a culture or subculture to accept their ecofacts as desirable. One of the most successful examples of such a process—which is sometimes described as making an ecofact environmental—occurred with the automobile. Today, the individual or family who does not have access to an automobile is deprived of many of the opportunities available in the American culture.

During the first fifty years of the twentieth century, it was possible successfully to make an ecofact environmental for the whole culture. This is becoming increasingly difficult today. It is now generally agreed by sociologists and politicians that the society is breaking down into subcultures, each of which has different ideas about desirable patterns of consumption. Marketing techniques to trick the economic mechanism today often aim at smaller groups. Much marketing today is designed to make a product environmental within a subculture and not within a total culture.

In addition to the subjective evaluation determined by cultural and subcultural norms, every individual has his own sets of purchasing priorities. Indeed, just as subcultures have been re-emerging as important determinants of consumption patterns, so individuals are increasingly asserting their own priorities rather than following blindly those of the groups around them. The desire to keep up with the Joneses still exists, but it is undoubtedly weakening.

In effect, the reassertion of subcultural and individual differences is limiting the power of the marketive to trick the economic mechanism over the long run—on the demand side. As groups and people apply their own subjective evaluation to the ecofacts they buy, it becomes less possible for marketives to create subjective cultural evaluations which force the purchase of a given ecofact.

Trickery of a culture, and indeed of the whole world, about its fundamental needs for the future is, of course, possible if sufficient resources are used to distort and suppress feedback. It is increasingly clear, however, that continuation of this process over an extended period of time will necessarily cause the end of human history.

Supply

Marketives usually benefit if they can decrease supply of the ecofacts they sell because the lower the supply, the higher the price will tend to be.

To make sense of this statement, we must define what we mean by an ecofact in this particular context: is it relevant to study gasoline as an ecofact, or should we be interested in a specific brand of gasoline? The answer to this question depends on the subjective attitudes of consumers. There is strong evidence today that ecofacts such as different brands of gasoline and cigarettes are in reality highly similar. They are differentiated primarily by advertising claims. An advertising expert once argued that his services were not needed if there was a real difference between ecofacts, because then anybody could write the advertisement; it was only when the essential ecofact difference had to be *invented* that his services were required!

If a marketive can successfully differentiate its cigarette or gasoline from that of others, it has created a sheltered market. The extent of this shelter will depend on the degree of preference; ideally, a marketive would like customers to buy its cigarettes or gasoline regardless of price difference or inconvenience. While such a result is seldom achieved, there is considerable evidence of very high levels of brand loyalty. But the degree of shelter is, of course, never total: people will change brands if the advantages are substantial. Indeed, people will change their consumption patterns far more broadly if forced to do so: for example, there are many ways of obtaining required food values, and communication can be substituted for transportation under many circumstances.

The attempt to create sheltered markets is not confined to the differentiation of ecofacts for consumer use. It can be effectively employed as a method of restricting the choice of purchasers of capital goods and industrial services to a particular marketive, if the purchaser can be convinced that only one marketive has the necessary qualifications and skills to create and/or supply what he needs. Sheltered markets of this type can be created most successfully if the prospective purchaser cannot obtain the information required to evaluate the skills and knowledge of the marketive and its personnel, and is forced to rely on public-relations statements.

Another technique for obtaining a privileged position is to possess the most qualified "professionals." The effectiveness of professionalism as a method of making ecofacts "unique" is greatly increased by developing a specialized jargon for each professional group, thus excluding all those who have not learned it.

In effect, most nonconsumer demand is no longer primarily determined on the basis of price, but by a subjective evaluation of which marketive is capable of carrying through the desired tasks. Marketives are often awarded contracts even if they are not the low bidder. This approach is, in fact, highly appropriate if the chosen marketive is likely to imagine, develop, design, and produce the most efficient ecofact for the described purpose. If, on the contrary, the marketive has gained its reputation through public relations—or direct use of power—the award of the contract will be highly inappropriate.

Our procedures for determining which marketive should carry out new tasks no longer work at all effectively. The key issue in the majority of cases is not cost but rather: "Will the chosen marketive develop the optimum response to a new problem?" A saving in initial design and production costs can only too easily be offset by expensive or dangerous aspects of the ecofact once it has been produced. (Failures of this type have been most publicized in the case of the military, but this does not mean that the problem is peculiar to them.) The only way to solve this problem is to discover ways to insure the availability of accurate information about real levels of competence to the purchaser.

The capacity of a marketive to control supply therefore usually depends on its ability to create a sheltered market. This is, of course, possible for natural monopolies and for monopolies which have been created by social and political decision making. It is also possible if sheltered markets have been created by advertising and public relations.

While the power of the marketive to manipulate price and profits through altering demand is declining, its power to alter supply conditions to its own advantage is still growing, for it is increasingly difficult to determine, even under the best of circumstances, which consumer ecofact is most satisfactory or which marketive should carry out a particular task. Indeed, the fragmentation of the market, which decreases the power of marketives to control demand, increases the problem of determining which marketive is most capable of supplying a particular ecofact. There are no automatic mechanisms working to prevent distortion here; we must therefore face directly the question of whether the present patterns of tricking the supply side of the market mechanism are compatible with effective control of economic—and, indeed, socioeconomic—systems.

LIMITATIONS ON DISTORTION

As the socioeconomy has become more dynamic, attempts at trickery on both the demand and the supply side have to alter their nature continuously if they are to act effectively. The thermostat analogy is still helpful here, but only to a limited extent. If we pack the thermostat with ice, this tricks the thermostat and the temperature of the room rises. This rise in temperature melts the ice more rapidly; new ice must be added to prevent the thermostat from "recognizing" the actual heat in the room. Similarly, automatic forces come into operation following successful trickery of the market mechanism; these make it necessary to expend more and more effort to preserve the trickery.

We must now recognize, however, two profound differences between a thermostat and a complex socioeconomic system. First, it is basically simple to continue to trick a thermostat for an indefinite period. For example, the thermostat could be placed in a refrigerator in the hot room, and it would no longer be necessary to worry about the ice melting. There is usually one feedback circuit in a thermostat, and it can normally be effectively immobilized.

Second, there is general agreement that a thermostat provides human beings with a desirable decision-making and feedback circuit. Although everyone in a room may not agree on the desirable temperature for that room, few would want to lose the opportunity of regulating the temperature at will.

Economic systems are different in nature: they have a very large number of feedback circuits. Some of these have been understood—for example, the patterns by which supply and demand interrelate with each other. In addition, we are sufficiently aware of the motivations and goals of some economic groupings to forecast accurately their reaction to certain developments: for example, unions will protest if the scale of payments to management and stockholders rises too rapidly compared with their own rewards.

There are, however, many potential feedback channels which will only be activated if certain economic or socioeconomic conditions develop. A good example of this process has been the largely unexpected development of support for the quaranteed income. When this issue started to be discussed in the early sixties, it appeared to many commentators that there were few feedback circuits which would support the idea and many which would oppose it. Time, however, has shown that this initial estimate was wrong: the need for reform of the welfare system, the need of governors of states and mayors of large cities for new sources of money, the growing pressures from the poor have combined to make the guaranteed income politically feasible.

On the other hand, unexpected negative feedback patterns can also emerge. At the beginning of the sixties, it appeared that the number of automobiles in the United States would continue to grow at increasing rates through the remainder of the century. Attitudes toward pollution, safety, and use of time have changed during the sixties, and the automobile is now no longer above criticism. It seems highly improbable that the number of automobiles in the United States will reach projected levels.

The existence of many potential feedback loops which can be called into existence by new situations would normally make it very difficult to trick socioeconomic systems for extended periods of time. There can be no doubt, however, that such trickery *was* accomplished for extended periods during the first two thirds of the twentieth century.

During the late industrial era, people believed that they should be "other-directed," to use David Riesman's expressive phrase. Industrial man believed, in effect, that the systems within which he lived were being effectively controlled by largely impersonal forces, and that his intervention would be ineffective, if not dangerous. He saw no reason to accept the responsibility for decision making; trends therefore continued in existing directions without counterpressures from new feedback channels.

This attitude extended specifically to the field of information movement. Many people were aware that they were participating in the movement of distorted information, but they felt no responsibility to correct the information, nor to try to change the system which led to the distortion.

The overall movement of the sixties can be understood largely in terms of the unclogging of feedback channels. Many views which had previously been unvoiced were now stated; many problems were brought out into the open. The short-run dangers of this process are, of course, obvious; they are treated in the last chapter, entitled "Short-Run Economic Issues." However, we must *also* recognize that the growth of feelings of responsibility about the necessity to insure correct decision making and accurate feedback throughout the society and the world are the fundamental hopeful indicators in Western societies at the present time.

The development of cybernetics theory and the subsequent discussion of methods of tricking the market enables us to reevaluate neoclassical theory. This is, in effect, a special case of the general theory of cybernetics. The neoclassicists perceived that the free-market system would work if there were no interruptions in the free flow of information required for efficient economic decision making.

Having examined how economic decision making is distorted in present conditions, we can now demonstrate that neoclassical theory must necessarily be unrealistic:

1. Neoclassical theory is valid only if there is no major change in conditions: as soon as man moved out of the agricultural era, increasingly dynamic change became inevitable.
2. Neoclassical theory is valid only if economic groupings have no power to distort information movement. In the industrial era, it is inevitable that economic groups both have power and use it to distort information for their own advantage.
3. Neoclassical theory demands that those making decisions be influenced only by economic factors or, in other words, behave as economic men. Such an assumption was relevant in the industrial era, when man's prime goal in the abundance regions was still to achieve the power to do what he wanted. As we enter the communications era and try to decide what we should do with the power we have achieved, we can no longer tolerate the concept of economic man. When making decisions and examining feedback we must consider all factors, not only the economic.

In effect, neoclassical theory becomes totally misleading as soon as we cease to be willing to study economics in a vacuum. The perfect information on economic matters required to validate the belief in a free-market system could be available only if we abandoned all other concerns. Today, the priorities of abundance-region societies have moved beyond the strictly economic to the socioeconomic; we must therefore give up the belief that free markets are, by themselves, effective means of distributing income and determining the proper uses of resources. This does not mean, of course, that we should fail to take advantage of the cybernetic elements available in any functioning market system, but only that we must recognize their limitations.

While this book is primarily concerned with the evolution in economic policy required by the obsolescence of neoclassical and neo-Keynesian theory, we must also perceive the meaning of the other critical difference between the thermostat as system and the total society as system.

The thermostat was created to fill a felt need; it is unlikely that any immediate changes will alter man's desire to be able to control the temperature in parts of his environment. The feedback pattern of the thermostat is well designed to achieve a desired human goal.

Societal reaction patterns, on the other hand, emerge from conditions in the past: they are based on needs which are no longer felt. Only too often the society uses old responses to react to fundamentally new conditions. Our long-run survival depends on our perception of the need for new feedback channels and the elimination of old ones which are no longer appropriate. The processes required for this purpose are quite different from those involved in the operation of a thermostat. As our society is controlled more and more completely by man himself, rather than by natural forces, the lead times required to take advantage of new potentials and to avoid disasters lengthen.

The insight gained by the neoclassicists can be updated in the following terms. Economies and societies cannot have accurate feedback or effective decision making so long as power is employed to distort information. The necessary societal commitment required for accurate feedback and effective decision making can only be secured if people recognize that the use of power to distort information is not in their own best interest, nor in that of their organization, nor in that of the society as a whole.

GROWTH IN SUPPLY

The two previous chapters have attempted to clear the ground of mismatched economic theories and economic facts. We are now able to consider the *real* factors which affect patterns of economic growth. It is, however, useful to recapitulate first those key statements in economics which we have found to be still valid.

All functioning systems, including economic ones, require effective decision making and accurate feedback. The market provides feedback channels for the economic system; automatic mechanisms are brought into play as supply, demand, and price alter. These mechanisms tend to slow down and often reverse the initial movement in demand, supply, or price. This is the valid core of neoclassical theory.

The obvious corollary to this is, of course, that blockage of any feedback channels, whether accidental or deliberate, leads to distortion of information and incorrect decisions. The farm programs of the last thirty-five years show, most dramatically, how efforts to improve the position of the farmer by controlling feedback channels create, over time, highly unsatisfactory economic and social patterns. Similar unsatisfactory patterns have followed from rent control.

While undistorted market mechanisms will tend to control microeconomic fluctuations in the economy, they will not lead to a balance between overall supply and demand. There is no automatic mechanism to insure the balancing of overall supply and demand in the economy. Carefully planned intervention is essential to balance growing potential supply with growing effective demand. This is the valid core of Keynesian and neo-Keynesian theory.

Having restated, briefly, the valid elements of neoclassical and neo-Keynesian analysis, we can define the inherent contradictions between them. *If the microeconomic system is to function most effectively, there should be no interruption of feedback along existing channels, for these serve to balance supply, demand, and price. If the macroeconomic system is, however, to continue to function effectively, there must be deliberate intervention, which aims to alter the present balance of the economy and which must therefore interfere with the effective functioning of existing market forces. The best functioning of the microeconomic system requires passivity; the best functioning of the macroeconomic system requires activity.*

One cannot today combine neoclassical and neo-Keynesian insights: in their present form they must be seen as thesis and antithesis, and they mix as unsuccessfully as oil and water. Only a fundamentally new synthesis can move us beyond the present contradictions.

We are now ready to take up the subject of economic growth. In this chapter, we shall examine the factors determining the rate of growth in supply; in the next chapter, we shall examine factors determining the rate of growth in demand.

EXPLAINING VARIATIONS IN THE RATE OF GROWTH IN SUPPLY

Any examination of rates of increase in supply must provide us with tools which will permit us to explain a reality that has so far received too little attention. Why do rates of growth throughout the world vary so substantially? Why has the rate of growth in Japan over the last decade been 14 percent, in Germany 7 percent, in America 5 percent and in Great Britain 3 percent (a rate that has also characterized many nations in the scarcity regions)?

Fortunately, we can specify the area in which we must search for an answer. It is obvious that the increase in productivity has not stemmed from increasing effort on the part of the individual; if anything, individuals work less vigorously than in the past. Rather, it has become possible to produce more ecofacts because of the information available to individuals and incorporated into the machines and machine systems with which they work. In order to discover the reason for differential rates of increase in productivity we must, therefore, examine the attitudes of societies toward that kind of education which will make men more productive and toward the introduction of more efficient machine systems which incorporate greater quantities of information.

The first explanation that springs to mind as one compares the various growth rates is the fact that the United States is more advanced technologically, and that therefore the remainder of the world can benefit immediately from her experience. Such a belief was, in fact, the mainspring of international economics for many decades: it was assumed that pressures would develop to equalize wealth and the availability of information. This thesis has proved faulty. If it were valid, the scarcity regions would presently have the highest rate of growth, for the extent of their lag behind the United States is greatest and they ought therefore to be able to take most advantage of the available information.

The scarcity regions, however, usually have low growth rates. We must seek another explanation. We can discover the correct answer by examining the implications of the work of communication theorists, who have made the obvious—but often ignored—point that effective transfer of a message requires the active cooperation of both sender and receiver. Each culture is particularly interested in certain types of "messages." The language, style, behavior, technology, and so on, of each culture determine which types of messages it can receive easily and accurately, which messages are distorted in transmission, and which cannot really be "heard" at all. In effect, the culture screens out certain patterns of thought and action by making them "unthinkable."

There is for every culture, at every historical point, a maximum feasible rate of increase in supply. This rate will never be attained, because no culture would devote all its energies to achieving more production. If we are to discover the actual forces which determine the rate of increase in supply, we must examine both the maximum potential rate of increase in supply and also cultural attitudes toward it.

Because discussions of the reasons for increasing supply have been confined to economists for so long—and because economists have assumed the essential existence of economic man and the critical importance of economic growth—it is difficult for those raised in Western cultures to grasp this reality. We are still inclined to believe, as an article of faith, that people will always try to achieve the maximum rate of economic growth that is possible.

But once we do succeed in examining the issue in this light, it is not difficult to understand why Japan and Germany have higher rates of increase in supply than Britain. Culturally, in Japan and Germany, priority is placed on a rise in individual standards of living, there is a characteristic passion for hard work and a willingness to pay the costs of competition. In addition, Germany and Japan are today activist cultures which had to seek new channels for self-expression after they were defeated in the mid-forties. They turned to economic growth as a way to demonstrate their continued viability and relevance. There is now some limited evidence which suggests that Germany is slowly changing its communication patterns and goals; it remains to be seen how long Japan will concentrate its efforts on achieving economic growth.

Great Britain, on the other hand, won the Second World War, and felt that it had thus proved the validity of its culture. Over the past twenty-five years, it has very largely refused to pay the costs required to benefit from the potential productivity increase available from new information. The United States is also presently changing its direction: at a time when new information permits far higher rates of growth in supply than before, many Americans no longer believe in the supreme importance of growth.

Economists cannot be relevant if they examine only the potential for growth in supply. They must also consider how much of the potential for growth in supply a given society wishes to achieve. In the remainder of this chapter we will discuss the two primary reasons why abundance regions are likely to continue to change their emphasis away from growth in supply. One is the implications of growth in supply on work availability; the other is the growing ecological concern. Together they threaten to create a neo-Luddite revolt: those involved would once again try to hamper technology and smash machine systems. Both of these trends and the drive to greater information availability are outside the short-run control of governments. The necessary balance of supply and demand cannot be effectively achieved by changing the rate of increase in supply.

THE JOB-WORK-PURPOSE QUESTION

We have already discovered that it is impossible to insure low levels of unemployment and price stability in a growth economy based on neo-Keynesian assumptions. We must now examine in more detail the reasons why it is unrealistic to try to preserve the goal of full employment in the long run and the implications of this reality.

It seems best to start from the challenge to the neo-Keynesian dogma launched early in the 1960s. At this time, a small group of people drew attention to the threat of unemployment and unemployability which they believed existed in the United States because of automation and growing cybernation. It was argued that the rapidly increasing complexity and skill of machine systems would so increase productivity that consumption would not keep up with production, and that machine systems would take the place of human beings in creating ecofacts. At first sight, the experience of the sixties appears to contradict completely this analysis and thus disposes of the question raised. The decade of the sixties closed with low levels of unemployment; to many, the prime problem of the future still appears to be an inability to find enough people for necessary jobs rather than a shortage of jobs.

The question of availability of jobs breaks down into two parts. The first is whether there will be adequate demand to take off the market all that is capable of being supplied. This was no problem in the late sixties: the combination of the Vietnam war and the growing use of power by marketives and unions insured excessive demand. The size of the gap between demand and supply was further increased as the government tried to introduce new social policies when demand was already overfull. We have seen that this pattern must change; we will deal with its implications in later chapters.

We shall therefore only examine here the second argument of those who challenged neo-Keynesianism in the early sixties. This second argument centered on the shifting balance of advantage between men and machines, as machines became "educated" faster than men. It was argued that human beings would lose their jobs to machine systems in increasing numbers. While our statistical techniques are not sufficiently accurate or sensitive to determine exactly what has occurred to the total number of unemployables, there is certainly no evidence of an overwhelming increase.

As a result, most economic commentators refuse to admit any threat from the problem of unemployability. However, the discussion in the last chapter shows that another explanation of the trend of the sixties is possible. It may well be that the feedback circuits which would have caused the predicted results were deliberately interrupted. If they were, and if pressures are still building up, we can predict not only that the initially expected results will occur but also that the speed of their eventual development will be even faster than was originally thought probable. In most circumstances, the longer an inevitable development is delayed, the more difficult it will be to control its threatening implications. Societal response mechanisms which might well have been adequate to deal with slowly changing conditions may be incapable of coping at a later date with the very rapid alteration resulting from deliberate interruption of feedback processes. There are three major factors which have prevented the unemployability crisis from becoming visible during the sixties:

1. Administrations committed themselves to finding jobs for all—even those with inadequate education, skills, and motivation. This led them to create incentives to force marketives to hire people who do not produce efficiently. In addition, increasing time was spent in retraining those who could find jobs; this kept them off the job market. Lack of human capacity to do productive work has been disguised by make-work jobs and ineffective training.
2. Marketives also felt an obligation to retain personnel—particularly senior people—even though they contributed nothing to the operation of the marketive. Parkinson's Law has operated with great effectiveness over the last decade; the work of bureaucracies has indeed expanded to fill time available: it has

been estimated that over 10 percent of many office and factory staffs could be fired without reducing production. In addition, Peter's Principle, which claims that people are promoted to the level of their inefficiency, has proved out fully.

3. The low levels of unemployment resulting from these first two measures reinforced the interruption of feedback. Marketives tried to hold on to all the labor they could find, the most skilled preferably, but if not, anybody who was available. In this situation, the gap between the attractive and unattractive worker was blurred.

As we enter the seventies, new feedback mechanisms are working to reverse past feedback patterns. First, the willingness of the Nixon Administration to reduce rates of growth and force a recession will lead marketives to release workers and managers whom they had previously retained to deal with any spurt in demand. Both the process of natural selection, and the union pattern of last-in-first-out, will result in larger firings of the inefficient.

Second, there will be growing social pressures arising from our increasing recognition of the need for more effective decision making to solve our social and ecological problems. It is becoming clear that decision making at a high level of efficiency will be required to create our future, as will a highly effective production and communication network. We shall no longer be able or willing to tolerate either the presence of managers who are incapable of constructive thought or the use of workers who limit or decrease the efficiency of production and communication systems. There has been a willingness to tolerate inefficiency so long as it only resulted in higher costs. This will not continue when we recognize that our survival is at stake.

What is an accurate description of the employment situation? *There is no chronic problem of unemployment, but there is a chronic problem of unemployability.* Any individual who can think and act creatively in any type of work need not fear unemployment; rather, he should be afraid of excessive work. On the other hand, both marketives and the total society are developing reasons why they cannot afford to hire or retrain those with insufficient education, skills, or motivation. Today, a worker's ignorance or a single careless action can easily cost a marketive more than his total annual wage or salary.

An unskilled, unmotivated, uneducated person will actually reduce production. He will do so partly by his own errors. More seriously, he will take up the time of those who are skilled, motivated, and knowledgeable. By so doing, he will prevent them from acting in ways which would have increased the efficiency of production or communication. The real cost of using the unskilled, unmotivated, and uneducated is the loss of time of those who are most valuable to the economy and society.

Our experience of remedial education and job retraining should have convinced us that there is no possible way in which we can avoid the consequences of *past* educational and socialization failures. Even if we were to commit ourselves immediately to preventing further failures, a large number of people would be unable to participate in tomorrow's patterns of production, distribution, and communication.

What reactions can we expect as this reality becomes clear? We can anticipate two prime patterns of feedback. First, human beings will fear for the loss of their income. We have, however, done much of the thinking necessary to find ways to compensate for this income loss. Second, there will be a profound psychological trauma for the vast majority of people. In Western societies, jobs are usually one of the prime sources of meaning for life; this is particularly true for many older workers in America.

The psychological threat is far more difficult to manage than the problem of finding new ways to distribute income rights. There are no quick and easy answers to this part of the problem; it is in this area that our delay in recognizing the reality of the unemployability issue will have the most serious consequences.

Some of the current proposals threaten to worsen the psychological problem. It has been argued, for example, that we should set up a system in which the government would serve as the employer of last resort. This suggestion obviously is invalid once one has understood the difference between unemployment and unemployability. It will be no easier for the government to find jobs for the unemployable than it will be for the private sector. It is the difference between the lack of skill today and the lack of demand in the thirties which creates a new situation. Only new conventions about work and meaningful activity will permit people who can no longer hold jobs to find continuing purpose in life.

THE ECOLOGICAL ISSUE

Economic growth has always been accompanied by inherent costs to mankind and to the environment, but the penalties of growth have been largely "invisible" in those regions which have achieved abundance. Indeed, one can argue that this invisibility was necessary if a culture was to be prepared to concentrate on economic growth and thus achieve abundance.

As the cost of economic growth to the environment and to people becomes clear, more and more decisions will be made in favor of the environment, with consequent limitation on growth in supply. *We shall perceive that environmental quality and growth in supply can be mutually incompatible.* Societies in the abundance-regions will certainly recalculate the balance of advantage between a good environment and further economic growth.

This chapter shows that the feedback mechanisms created by abundance have already undercut the basic structures of the industrial era. In the industrial era, man aimed to produce as much as he could. In the cybernetic era, man is abandoning this industrial-era goal, and he is trying to discover what he should do with the power he created during the industrial era. As understanding of this spreads throughout the abundance regions, the percentage of effort devoted to securing further increases in supply will certainly decline.

Two forces, however, may act to limit the rate of decline in supply and could actually reverse it. First, the information available to us is now growing so fast that even if we devote a lesser proportion of societal energy to achieving growth in supply we may still achieve the same, or greater, rates of growth.

Second, as we discover the true meaning of abundance, we shall perceive the urgent needs of the scarcity regions to which we have so far been oblivious. At this point, we shall be prepared to recognize the high priority of increasing supply on a global level.

It should be noted that the aspects which have been examined in this chapter are different from those normally employed in discussions of ways of increasing supply. It therefore seems necessary to mention briefly why certain issues have not been discussed.

1. Increase in working population. It has normally been assumed in economic theory that an increase in working population would increase supply. We can now see that this is not necessarily so. The relationship only holds if the incoming labor force has been appropriately educated.

    If the education has not been appropriate, there may actually be a decrease in available supply. This may be true whether the workers are employed or remain unemployed. If they are employed, they can be so inefficient that their net production will be negative both because of their mistakes and because of the time they take up of people who could be more effectively employed. If they remain unemployed, they will cut into the surplus which could otherwise have been used to buy machines and machine systems.

2. Increase in machines and machine systems. It has normally been assumed that an increase in machines and machine systems would increase the pace of economic growth. We can now see that this is not necessarily so. It is true only if the machines and machine systems installed have had incorporated into them the appropriate level of information. If they have not, there may actually be a decrease in supply. Introduction of insufficiently or excessively complex machine systems may actually slow the rate of increase in supply by using too much or too little of the cooperating factors of production, such as skilled workers and management.

In effect, therefore, increases in working population and increases in the availability of machines and machine systems are not good or bad in themselves but only in terms of their information content. As we have already seen, the key factor in determining the rate of growth in supply is the ability of the society to perceive relevant information, and the decision of the society as to the amount of effort it will use to bring about growth in supply. This decision will be reflected in educational and capital equipment policies.

GROWTH IN DEMAND

The last chapter examined the factors affecting growth in supply. We have seen that in abundance regions, the potential for growth in supply is continuing to increase, but that cultural attitudes are changing so that there is a widening gap between potential increases in supply and actual increases in supply.

In effect, governments have little power to manipulate supply factors: alterations in both potential and actual increases in supply are determined primarily by long-run cultural trends. The short-run balancing of the economy which Keynes has shown to be necessary must therefore be carried out by changing the factors which affect levels of demand. We shall examine these factors systematically, determining which of them are open to short-run manipulation for purposes of balancing supply and demand.

Population Size

It is generally agreed that population size is one of the major determinants of demand. Each addition to the population consumes, at a minimum, the food, clothing, and shelter required for survival. In addition, families set their living standards and try to maintain them. Thus, a child born into a rich family creates a high level of demand for additional ecofacts. Increases in population therefore imply quasi-automatic increases in demand.

There have been many attempts to influence birth rates throughout the world. The evidence today is fairly conclusive: birth rates change with cultural attitudes rather than with financial incentives. Indeed, whatever the degree of flexibility in the birth-rate, it is obviously impossible to affect short-run demand significantly by changing the population size.

Waste

Some twelve years ago, an article in Harper's Magazine jokingly suggested that it was the American acceptance of waste that had made it possible to achieve American standards of living. As we have come to understand the implications of neo-Keynesian policies, the correctness of this statement has become obvious, and it has become, at the same time, far from funny. The American economy has been abundant because of waste. The declining willingness to tolerate waste poses major questions for the future balancing of supply and demand.

1. War. John Maynard Keynes once stated that industrial-era economies have achieved full employment only in times of war, in preparation for it, or in recovery from it. This statement, while perhaps not entirely true, serves to remind us of the key role that war has played in creating periods of prosperity, including our most recent boom in the late sixties. (The morality and justice of any war is not being considered here. From an economic point of view war is waste: ecofacts are destroyed without economic return or individual satisfactions.)
2. Accelerated obsolescence. There has so far been little attempt to design ecofacts which would have an optimum life period. Nor, in general, have ecofacts been designed to minimize re-

pairs. Marketives have failed to design for optimum lives, because they have desired a built-in replacement market and they have been concerned that ecofacts that were too well produced would put them out of business. The reality of this situation has always been one of the factors keeping up demand. Its impact is increasing as people find it impossible to discover competent repairmen who will mend their malfunctioning ecofacts. Rather than pay high service fees for inadequate work, they prefer to throw away an ecofact and repurchase.
3. Pollution. We are just beginning to understand how much of our present production and activity is designed to deal with the negative effects of previous activities. As we turn toward solving our ecological problems, one of the most urgent technical reforms is to find ways to separate out the costs of reversing negative outputs. Today, we count in Gross National Product not only the minerals we mine but also the cost of reversing the pollution resulting from their extraction. We shall only be able to have a clear picture of the development of our economy in the seventies if we separate out negative and positive inputs and outputs.

Waste is still a major method used to boost the Gross National Product (GNP). It is, however, under increasing attack. There is growing understanding that war must be abolished if mankind's survival is to be insured; that accelerated obsolescence and pollution will lead to the destruction of the environment on which our survival depends; and that decent standards of work and service must be revived. In effect, therefore, there are long-run pressures to reduce waste. In addition—and even more critically in the context of this chapter—it will be increasingly difficult for governments to manipulate the degree of waste in order to achieve short-run balancing in the economy.

Capital Expenditures

Governments often try to balance the economy by introducing measures which change the amount of money being spent on machines and machine systems. Thus, for example, a special depreciation allowance will lead marketives to increase the amount they spend on equipment, for its net cost to them will be lowered.

There is, however, a feedback process which prevents such policies from providing a satisfactory answer to the neo-Keynesian balance problem. Given present circumstances, the new machines and machine systems installed will necessarily incorporate more information. Their production will therefore lead to a more rapid increase in supply than would have occurred in the absence of the policy. Over the long run, therefore, any government policy which increases incentives to buy capital equipment, which will necessarily be more productive, will widen the already existing gap between supply and demand.

In effect, governments will only succeed in masking temporarily the basic problem: a lack of final demand. If the lack of final demand continues, marketives will eventually find their stock of machines and machine systems grossly excessive, and they will drastically cut back their expenditures on capital equipment. This will necessarily lead to a severe recession.

Increasing Tastes

The major demand factor balancing ever-rising available supply in recent years has been the desire of people to obtain more ecofacts. This pattern has become so pervasive that we no longer perceive its extent nor the fact that increasing tastes are neither inevitable nor necessarily desirable. Most of us have ceased to observe that we live primarily in a "selling" world designed to pressure us to consume more every year. In reality, the commerical message itself has become environmental; the feedback processes of the total society have been tricked into supporting selling messages.

In effect, a very substantial part of our information-moving processes would collapse without their support by commercial messages.

Under these circumstances, there is no need for direct pressures to insure the environmentality of selling. It is inevitable that the mass media will be structured as the most effective salesmen rather than as accurate information movers. (Our only hope of immediate alleviation of this situation stems from the new studies on the effect of commercial clutter and advertising overload coupled with the reality of dull programing. These could force some changes. Any significant alteration will have to await the realization by the society that accurate feedback and efficient decision making are essential for our survival.)

Another effective feedback loop which has helped to make sure that selling messages remain pervasive is the economics profession. It still proclaims as an article of faith that there is no limit to wants. Strangely, however, economists bring no evidence to prove this statement. Indeed, existing economic theory, correctly applied, shows that as the quantity of available ecofacts increases there will be a tendency to pay more attention to other factors, such as free time.

The latter half of the sixties has seen the beginning of an attack on the environmental nature of selling. Many feedback channels have been developing which challenge the constant pressure toward higher consumption. A consumers' revolt is developing. Its immediate targets are shoddy products, accelerated obsolescence, and everything implied by the caution: "Let the buyer beware." Behind the growing forces lies a deeper motivation. There is a growing belief among many people—particularly the young—that ecofacts are a means to an end rather than an end in themselves.

Industrial-era man saw purpose in toil and consumption themselves. He obtained satisfaction from his job and the ecofacts available to him. In the industrial era, there was no effective concept of "enough." In the cybernetic era, the concept of "too much" is as perceivable as the concept of "too little." New and very substantial barriers are therefore rising against any governmental policies which would force still faster increases in tastes as the method of balancing supply.

Indeed, there are inherent reasons which force us to cease promoting new tastes today. We can see this by analyzing the process of promoting new tastes. New tastes emerge when new information is brought to the potential consumer of the ecofact. At the very best, even assuming that the information is as accurate and honest as it can be made, its absorbtion and understanding require time. The time used in this way cannot be used in other ways—for example, in gaining understanding of the overall process of change taking place at this time.

In most cases, however, commercial messages are not intended to present information without bias. They are formulated to attempt to influence the emotions, to trick the potential consumer, and they may even be totally false. Commercials are often designed to introduce insecurities and to lead people to believe in unreal necessities.

The personal costs of this system have been examined so often that there is no need for repetition. It is important to understand, however, that there is a systematic danger when there is effective trickery of the total socioeconomy, whether haphazard or deliberate. In such cases, the commercial desires of certain marketives come to dictate the social direction of the earth. This process, if it should be continued for any lengthy period, will necessarily tend to destroy the capacity of the earth to support man, for it would work to prevent the required reconstruction of mankind's priorities.

In the communications era we are now entering, man creates his own future by the information he circulates. We should not permit marketives to use their power to promote sales rather than to help create a more accurate feedback and efficient decision-making network. This does not mean that we can, or should, abolish the future-creation function of marketives: this would be both unnecessary and unsatisfactory. Rather, we must demand that marketives evaluate their future-creation activities in terms of the goals of the total society.

The process of manipulating tastes can no longer, therefore, be used as a short-run method of influencing demand.

Government Expenditures

It appeared for a brief period during the sixties that the American people were prepared to see the government balance supply and demand through changes in federal spending, and in fiscal and monetary policies. In Europe, government spending has been an acceptable method of balancing the economy over a longer period of years. But throughout the world, a movement against big government is now gathering strength. Is this movement merely evidence of reaction against the new, or is there sound reasoning behind it?

It is now generally agreed that there are fundamental social ills which must be relieved and that the solution of these will require the availability of much of the most highly skilled manpower and the most advanced machine systems over coming decades. This reality is hardly challenged today; the question now in dispute is what means can best be used to mobilize manpower and machine systems for these purposes.

President Kennedy campaigned on a platform of increasing government programs and expenditures to eliminate social ills. For three years, Congress refused to pass the most significant parts of the program. After his assassination, however, a passion of national concern and guilt led the American people to grant President Johnson all that Kennedy had asked, and indeed more.

From the vantage point of the seventies, it can now be seen that the orgy of national guilt, and subsequent legislation, is to prove the highest cost of the assassination of President Kennedy. It led the Congress and the country to try to solve the new problems of the communication era with the outdated tools derived from a liberal philosophy. Large-scale government bureaucracies were used to tackle problems for which they were inherently unsuited. In effect, dying feedback processes were temporarily resuscitated and the growth of new feedback loops suppressed.

If the assassination had not occurred, the problems of our new era of cybernetics would have been borne in on the society gradually over the decade. We would have used the sixties to engage in new thinking and new institution building. The result would have been less dramatic—and dangerous—than the violent imbalances with which we enter the seventies.

Central governments are presently organized bureaucratically. Their inherent structuring makes it impossible for them to handle the problems and possibilities of the cybernetic era: feedback circuits within and between bureaucracies *inherently* distort information. We must find fundamentally new organizational styles if we are to deal with the real problems of the present time. This need is increasingly sensed, if not fully understood, by citizens who are demanding decentralization of decision making.

In present circumstances, power held by the government results in distortion of information for the same reasons and in the same way as power held by any other group. One of the primary goals of federal bureaucracies and the individuals in them is survival. We must, therefore, expect government bureaucracies to distort information to ensure their survival. But this situation, as we have seen, is intolerable in today's conditions, when mankind's decisions control the direction in which it will move: incorrect information must necessarily lead to ineffective decisions.

The government's power to affect the balance of supply and demand by changing its spending and taxing policies is diminishing as citizens discover that it possesses no magical key to solving current problems. People are no longer willing to accept rapid increases in government taxation aimed at supporting additional government programs.

What, then, of the alternative route? If fiscal policies are no longer acceptable, is it possible to balance supply and demand by adjusting monetary policies and rates of interest? This was the emphasis in 1969: money was very tight, and interest rates were driven up to exceptionally high levels.

We have been retesting monetary policy in a situation where there is too much demand. Keynes proved as long ago as the thirties that low rates of interest will not normally increase demand when supply is excessive and when demand needs to be increased. The lack of confidence generated by such a situation will prevent most people from being interested in investment even if money is widely available and rates of interest are low.

We are now discovering that restrictive monetary policies to limit demand must be avoided because of their highly distortive effects. First, it is clear that those who have privileged access to money managers will gain more than their fair share of limited financial resources under these conditions. Rates of interest are therefore a very blunt instrument, even when one is concerned only with the economic value of investments. In today's circumstances, when we must be interested in socioeconomic effects, high rates of interest are profoundly distortive of feedback channels and act to prevent effective decision making.

CHANGING THE DISTRIBUTION OF INCOME

We have now examined all the ways usually proposed to balance supply and demand and have found them to be ineffective. Does this mean that the need to balance supply and demand cannot be met?

There is one other way which we must now consider, but which is generally ignored in most discussions. One of the most clearly established economic relationships is between level of income and level of savings. On the average, the poor save nothing and even dissave. The rich save; normally, the higher their income, the more they save.

Such a relationship is, of course, explainable in common-sense terms. Those who are poor necessarily have urgent needs for ecofacts. Many of the poor will spend all the money they have and will also go into debt. Saving is a residual quantity: it is what is left over. Even if the poor tried to save, unexpected events would probably prevent them from doing so successfully. On the other hand, those who are rich have lesser subjective needs for additional ecofacts in many cases, and therefore fail to spend all their income.

The level of demand can therefore be immediately and significantly affected by changing the distribution of income. If one changes the distribution of income toward greater equality, this reduces the amount of saving and thus increases demand relative to supply. If, on the other hand, one changes the distribution of income toward inequality, this increases saving and thus reduces demand relative to saving.

In reality, of course, there has been little attempt to change patterns of income distribution in the United States. Despite government measures of all types during the twentieth century, the after-tax percentage of income going to the top 20 percent of the population and to the bottom 20 percent has not altered significantly. Loopholes in apparently progressive income-tax structures have been exploited most effectively by the rich, while income has not been transferred in such a way that it reaches the very poor. This failure to change significantly degrees of income inequality has been intellectually supported by the neoclassical theory, which "proved" that each person received the value of his production; it could therefore always be argued that it was unjust to take income away from an individual.

We have already seen, however, that this neoclassical analysis is not valid. In a world in which information is able to be distorted, the largest incomes go to those who have the power to distort information most effectively for economic ends. The present distribution of income follows the distribution of power in the society rather than being based on contributions to production.

This view is, of course, not accepted today, and it will take time for it to be understood. Let us assume, however, for the moment that the view has been adopted and that the society has become willing to act upon it. We would then possess an effective means of balancing supply and demand: we would simply alter the degree of income inequality in the society. If demand fell short of supply, we would decrease inequality; if supply fell behind demand, we would increase inequality.

As the long-run trend in the abundance regions is for supply to run ahead of demand, we shall need to reduce income inequality over time. In the process of moving toward income equality, we shall not only balance increased supply with increased demand, but we shall also act to reduce the degree of distortion in information movement.

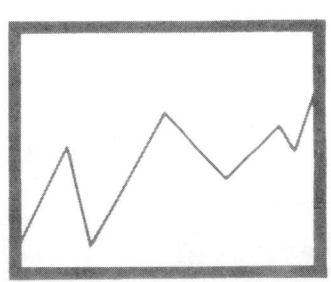

INTERMISSION

THE
ISSUES
DEFINED

We have now reached the halfway point of this book, and can summarize what has been said about the present economic system.

The economic system operates on the basis of fundamental distortion of information for the benefit of those who have power. This distortion is designed to create artificial scarcity and to influence the distribution of resources in favor of those who possess power. All power interventions have become dysfunctional in the light of our need for accurate feedback and effective decision making. The only feasible *and* desirable method of balancing supply and demand is to alter the distribution of income. This measure is appropriate, because, as we shall see in the next chapter, it operates to prevent distortion of information.

It is critical that we perceive at this point the magnitude of the change in thinking and policy that is being proposed. Societies should never make a more fundamental change if a lesser one will suffice. Before going on to explore the steps which should be taken to change levels of income inequality, we must make sure that no economic policy presently being proposed would avoid the need for such total change.

What proposals are being advanced to balance potential supply with growing demand? The officially stated position of the Administration at the present time is that it will eliminate the present imbalances by restraining the economy sufficiently to break the inflationary spiral without, however, causing excessive unemployment. If this were possible, we could continue with present patterns; we have, however, already seen that we will suffer from either excessive unemployment or excessive inflation or both until we alter present patterns of belief and action.

As understanding of this reality develops, the Administration will be forced to choose between permitting the rate of inflation to increase or permitting unemployment to increase. Both political and economic factors make acceptance of high rates of inflation unlikely. The other alternative is no more satisfactory. Permitting unemployment to rise to the level necessary to stop inflation would lead to major social unrest. In addition either approach would imply the end of neo-Keynesian policies, which are based on the attempt to maintain *both* low unemployment rates and stable prices.

If low rates of unemployment and stable prices cannot be achieved within an uncontrolled economy, why not use wage and price controls? The answer to this question can be provided both from neoclassical and cybernetic theory. The ever-increasing distortion of feedback resulting from wage and price controls would necessarily lead to a steadily worsening situation.

We have seen that the market, if its operation is not distorted, provides effective feedback systems to adjust supply to demand. We have also seen that there is a wide range of techniques being used to prevent market forces from being effective. Given the necessity for accurate feedback and effective decision making, we have learned that we must move away from techniques which distort the operation of the economic thermostat.

Introduction of price and wage controls by the government would fatally delay the necessary adjustments in the economy. Instead of commencing the urgently necessary process of eliminating the distortions which have already been built into the economic system through past business, labor, and government pressures, we would complicate and aggravate them. Government distortion of feedback mechanisms can have particularly serious consequences. The complexity of the present society insures that a large number of feedback channels tend to develop to prevent the continuous use of power by labor and management to distort market mechanisms. Government bureaucracies, however, have significant *continuing* power to prevent existing feedback channels from operating and to prevent new feedback channels from coming into existence.

Fortunately, at the present time there is little apparent support among economists for wage and price controls. If the information model contained in this volume is understood, we shall be able to continue to prevent the mistake of moving still farther away from the free-market system.

The final and most rapidly growing argument of economists is less obviously incorrect, and indeed starts from one of the beliefs which lies behind this volume: that the government has tried to do too much. It is being argued that economists should abandon their attempt to "fine tune" the economy through manipulation of tax rates, government expenditures, and so on. Those making this argument, often called "monetarists," state that the appropriate method of insuring continuing balance is to increase the availability of money in the economic system at a basically set rate, regardless of the fluctuations of the economy. It is argued that monetary policy of the sixties, an attempt to adjust rates of monetary increase on a "counter cyclical" basis, by increasing supply at a faster rate during recessions and at a slower rate in booms, is ineffective, for it inevitably sets up feedback patterns which lead to inflationary policies followed by recessions.

The implications of the policy of constant monetary increase are startling. In effect, it is once again being argued that the economy will look after itself if only it is left alone; the "invisible hand" of Adam Smith has again appeared. But we know from earlier arguments that it is impossible to rely on an invisible hand in present conditions: a competitive invisible hand would only achieve the necessary accurate feedback and effective decision making if:

1. There were no deliberate information distortion, and, by extension, power were not used to distort information.
2. We were only concerned with the direction of the economic, rather than the socioeconomic, system.

As these conditions are not fulfilled, the proposed return to reliance on an invisible hand is dangerously irrelevant.

In effect, the monetarists are proposing that we act as though the theoretical world of the neoclassicists were the real world. The proposals of the monetarists would not only minimize intervention in the macroeconomic system; they would also return to the attempt to eliminate all sources of power in the economy. They would ignore the lessons we learned in the late nineteenth and early twentieth centuries which showed that some forms of power are more easily controllable than others. The monetarists would tear down the carefully constructed system of countervailing power between unions, marketives, and governments without putting anything in its place.

The monetarists have seen only one part of current problems and possibilities. They have perceived that the vast majority of the power mechanisms we have developed are unsatisfactory and that we must return to a greater reliance on free market forces. They have not understood that in order to be able to do so we must develop new *systems* of societal security which would be effective in the absence of jobs for all, nor have they considered how to eliminate *all* the information distortion resulting from the availability of power.

Having eliminated the proposals presently being made to insure a balance between supply and demand, we can now conclude that it is necessary to discover how to change the degree of inequality in the distribution of resources. We must therefore examine the implications of making deliberate changes in the distribution of resources and explore the other policies required to balance supply and demand and to promote accurate feedback and effective decision making.

Before doing so, however, we must take explicit note of the fact that discovering the right pattern of action and insuring its adoption are, of course, two different problems. We "knew" in the thirties that the way to end the Great Depression of the period was to increase effective demand. Given the standard of living of the time, this could have been achieved in several ways. However, the attitudes of economists, bankers, businessmen, and the general public made it impossible to apply this knowledge to the actual situation. Policy measures follow changes in attitudes; they do not precede them. Education is the first step in insuring the introduction of new policies. Politicians today almost always follow public opinion rather than lead it.

Is it probable that education will lead people to accept fundamentally new economic policies? An examination of the possibilities or probabilities of achieving the necessary education of the public is outside the scope of this book. It is enough to state in this context that education necessarily precedes policy formation.

It might, however, be usefully added that the need for fundamental reexamination exists in all policy areas, and that one of the most serious problems now facing the total society is our failure to develop new ways to meet this need for reeducation. It has been assumed both that the public will acquiesce in fundamental alterations of their life-style without understanding the need for them and that politicians will vote for new policies without public backing. Both of these views are faulty. We must discover what techniques can be used to provide information about the new realities to the total society so that they can determine the course they wish to follow.

Cybernetic and communication theory is relevant here. We are only now coming to understand the obvious point that constructive change in behavior involves the effective transfer of accurate information from one person to another in such a way that it changes views about "self-interest." This process requires that:

1. There be no attempt deliberately to distort information.
2. There be a common perception of reality which permits the sender and receiver of the information to understand the message in the same way.
3. Sender and receiver are interested in making the effort to transfer the message.

The insights of communication theory have as yet been little used in restructuring societies to promote understanding of required new policies. They have, however, been taken up in management rhetoric, although not always in management practice. Managements are rethinking required organization structures as it becomes understood that accurate feedback and effective decision making cannot be achieved in a hierarchical, authoritarian system. The reasons are obvious. Nobody wishes to bring bad news to his boss: information moving within a hierarchical system must necessarily be distorted. Language patterns at higher and lower levels of the hierarchy are usually profoundly different; distortion of messages as they move between levels are therefore inevitable. An increasingly small proportion of those working in hierarchical organizations are committed to their work; they therefore will not make the necessary effort to communicate effectively.

The art of management is increasingly perceived as the skill of promoting the most effective communication. This can occur only in a self-organizing system, where those involved have the freedom to restructure their activities and communication patterns for maximum relevance and competence. Strangely, the necessity for more effective communication is often misunderstood as a further move toward an authoritarian society. The argument above makes it clear that this view is incorrect. In fact, we are moving away from structural authority based on position to sapiential authority based on knowledge.

Neither accurate feedback nor effective decision making is possible without this move from structural to sapiential authority. Such a change is a necessity if we are to survive in our new situation in which mankind has so much power that his decisions are shaping the world in which he will live in coming decades and centuries.

How are we to achieve the shift between the industrial era and the communications era? As we study this problem, it becomes clear that we do not presently possess the freedom necessary to move out of the industrial era; we are indeed trapped between two eras, one dead and the other struggling to be born.

We shall examine how to escape from the constraining influence of neo-Keynesian policies in the next chapter: at this point we shall briefly consider the general problem. Mankind's previous transitions between eras have been made on the basis of shifting leadership. The necessary alterations in cultural norms occurred as one tribe, city, or nation lost power and influence and another gained it. For example, Spain, which had adapted to an earlier life-style, lost out to Great Britain when Great Britain was already moving toward the industrial era.

Past changes between eras have inevitably involved the decline of one society and the rise of another. Because the elements in every culture are very closely interconnected, and because change in one aspect of a culture therefore always brings about change in many others, adaption to new conditions is necessarily difficult. In addition, a culture or group which has been successful at a particular period of history becomes overconfident: it fails to perceive the reality of change, and persists in believing that its culture is relevant, and indeed successful, until its decline cannot be reversed.

Periods of shifting leadership have historically been accompanied by chaos and confusion. Indeed, there was often considerable violence, as the declining power used what force it could still assemble to try to crush those powers that were challenging it. Effective, forward-looking decision making was therefore impossible during these periods.

It is for this reason that we must seek new methods for carrying through the shift between the industrial and the cybernetic eras. As we must make highly intelligent decisions in the remainder of the century if we are to insure our survival, we cannot tolerate the confusion and violence inherent in a struggle for leadership. In a very real sense, therefore, our situation has become ahistorical.

Mankind has never before planned for a total change in his culture. As readers examine the proposals made in the next chapters, they must therefore control carefully their emotions. The first step is to decide whether a case for fundamental change in the economic system has been made. *If it has not, the rest of the book is irrelevant. If it has, the obvious reaction that the changes suggested are too large to be feasible must be fought back. The need is to find out how change of this magnitude can be achieved in the future.*

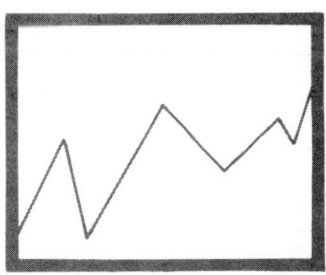

ECONOMIC
POLICIES
IN THE SEVENTIES

POLICY MEASURES TO CHANGE THE DISTRIBUTION OF RESOURCES

The distribution of resources within a culture depends on the values of that culture. Industrial-era countries have believed that there were immutable economic laws which determined the distribution of resources. We have now seen that this is a myth. We must therefore determine for ourselves what norms of societal security we are going to use to determine the distribution of resources in the future.

It may help us if we start by looking at the norms which operated in previous cultures. In hunting and gathering tribes, the system of societal security was usually based on the group which lived together. In good times, the whole group ate well; in bad times, the group ate less well; and in disastrous times, the group would die out. Loyalty was to the group. In the worst possible circumstances, the weakest in the group would be abandoned or killed. Even the strongest individual would not try to save his life at the expense of the group.

In agricultural societies, one prime pattern of societal security was through the family—usually an extended family containing far more members than is normal in the West: not only man, wife, and children but sisters and brothers, aunts and uncles, and so on. This system of societal security was based on the continuity of the family: the young were cared for when they were helpless, and they were then expected to care for the old when they could no longer work. Life and the capacity for work were a "gift" of the extended family, and those who did well felt that it was right for their relatives to share their resources. Those who did badly did not feel demeaned by taking aid from those who did well. Other agricultural societal security systems were based on positions within a tribe. In such tribes, people received resources on the basis of their ability to fill the necessary roles within the tribe, but there was less concern for individual lives than there normally was in hunting and gathering tribes.

The mobility associated with industrial societies broke up the extended family. Individuals moved out on their own. They felt that their achievements stemmed from their own skills and activity. In most cases, they continued to recognize a responsibility to look after their wife and minor children, but they felt less and less responsibility for their brothers and sisters, their aunts and uncles and, increasingly, their parents. The survival of individuals became dependent very largely on their own efforts. For a considerable period the basic philosophy of Western cultures justified this situation.

In effect, the central ideology of the industrial era is the possibility, and indeed the philosophical desirability, of each individual being able to stand alone. Ayn Rand is the modern philosopher of this school. During the nineteenth century, the surviving elements of agricultural societal security systems hid the full consequences of this philosophy, while the open frontier gave it some validity.

After the end of the First World War, both agricultural societal security schemes and the open frontier had essentially vanished in the abundance regions. Men could look after themselves only if they could find jobs. Keynes's understanding that the economic system would not automatically balance supply and demand and that there was a possibility of a chronic shortage of jobs therefore threatened to damage fatally the fundamental philosophic underpinnings of the industrial era. If a man could be unemployed through no fault of his own, it becomes highly unreasonable to believe in a system which demands that the individual be held responsible for the consequences of his actions and failures to act.

Keynes's understanding forced rethinking. *It became clear that the survival of the philosophic basis of the industrial era, with its belief in competition, could only be insured if the society would act to guarantee jobs for all.* This reality explains the unexpectedly rapid domination of Keynesian thinking, first in Europe and then in the United States. It was less effort for an industrial-era culture to conserve its philosophic assumptions and accept fundamental change in its operation rather than to bring upon itself the necessity for total rethinking. In effect, we packed the social thermostat with ice rather than examine the situation to discover whether the feedback circuits we were employing were useful in our new situation.

The willingness of industrial-era cultures to accept change in operating styles in order to prevent change in philosophic assumptions has bought less time than might have been expected. We have already seen how new feedback circuits have come into existence and are creating major pressures against neo-Keynesian policies. Environmental concerns, as well as neo-Luddite and consumer revolts, will undoubtedly force major changes in coming years.

It is, however, still far from certain that the direction and nature of forthcoming changes will be desirable unless we become clearer on the nature of the central issue. We are confronted with the need for reconsideration of the way in which we shall provide societal security for all. We cannot continue the neo-Keynesian techniques for the reasons given in the first part of this volume. It will, however, be possible to abandon the neo-Keynesian attempt to minimize unemployment and to provide incomes for most people on the basis of their wages and salaries only after we have developed a different societal security system capable of making resources available to all those in the society.

If we had to start the discovery and development of such a new system from the beginning, we would certainly not have time to create it. There is, fortunately, an alternate source of societal security which is far more developed than we are usually prepared to admit. Indeed, there is surprising support for the alternative, despite the fact that it cuts across our industrial-era philosophy.

The belief that people should manage all the shocks of life through their own efforts was always more acceptable to writers and philosophers than to those who had to live with its consequences. Those who have supported the philosophy of individual responsibility most strongly are usually those cushioned against the more unpleasant shocks of life: they were unlikely to be unemployed, and they had the wealth to deal with problems of sickness and property damage.

The ordinary citizen has always needed to find protection from events which damaged his interests through no fault of his own. As the agricultural patterns of societal security ceased to be operative, individuals increasingly organized service and friendly clubs which came to the aid of their members in times of death, sickness, and damage to property. Later, people took advantage of the ever-wider range of private insurance policies available to protect them from catastrophes. Still later, political pressures developed for government schemes to provide income during unemployment, disability, and old age.

During the last hundred years, while our attention has been concentrated on the doctrine of individual responsibility, we have been developing a parallel societal security system based on group sharing of risks. The group can, in theory, be large or small, but increasingly schemes are backed by the total resources of the country. A collapse in any major portion of our societal insurance pattern, whether public or private, is no longer "thinkable."

We are still largely unaware of the fundamental implications of this insurance societal security system. We have disguised its reality by arguing that it amounts only to a reallocation of funds, and that the total sums paid out are based on actuarial principles. In other words, it is suggested that the group as a whole does not get out of this type of societal insurance more than it puts into it; each individual may choose to share his risks with others, but he is still ultimately responsible for himself.

In reality, of course, the very reason that government entered the realm of unemployment, old-age, and health insurance—thus acting against the industrial-era myth—was precisely that much of the task of providing societal security could not be handled on an actuarial basis. For example, there is no way in which adequate insurance can be obtained for the old without the assistance of the general revenues of the federal government. Half-hearted efforts are still being made to describe the government's payments under the "social security" program as being actuarially based. In reality, almost everybody is receiving benefits far above those which could be justified on an actuarial basis. Given the fact that Congress tends to increase benefits each election year, this will certainly continue to be true.

This is, of course, both appropriate and just. Because of the continuing rise in standards of living, and also because of inflation, the average annual income earned by an individual over his lifetime will normally be far below the amount he earns in the year he leaves his job. Thus, even if he puts aside the maximum financially prudent amount for private, actuarially-based life insurance during the time he works, he will necessarily find that his income is excessively low on retirement. The only way this shortfall can be made up is by payments from the generation now working to the generation which is retired.

Such payments are totally justified. The reason the working generation can benefit from its present high standard of living is *not*, as we have seen, mainly due to its effort. Rather, it is due to the information which has been created and incorporated in men's minds and in machine systems. The worker of today has no right to claim that he should keep all his production; he should share it with those who helped create it. This is only a special case of the theory stated earlier. The distribution of wealth depends upon power. Our society has provided little power to the old; their share of available resources has therefore been limited.

In the seventies, a severe clash between the two societal security systems now existing is inevitable. On the one hand, we have a system which involves the differential distribution of resources based on the power of groups to distort information for their own purposes. This system cannot be permitted to continue, for it is based on the deliberate distortion of information. The only available alternative is a society in which we meet our need for a societal security system by an extension of the present patterns of public and private insurance. When we do this, we can accomplish three tasks at once. First, we deal *directly* with the needs for resources of all those in the society. Second, we possess the instrument for balancing supply with demand. Third, we can begin to undercut the present sources of distortion in feedback.

Let us look briefly at the objections normally made to this method:

Objection: We are giving up a system which has worked well for one which is untried. *Answer:* We are not voluntarily giving it up: the very successes of the industrial era have caused us to move into the cybernetic era with the necessity of new norms. *Objection:* We will abolish incentives. *Answer:* Empirical studies show that present incentive patterns are working increasingly badly. If we are to insure that the necessary work will get done, we shall have to discover new incentive patterns more suitable for the era we are entering.

Objection: The change is politically infeasible. *Answer:* Our societal security system is far more developed than we fully understand; there is also far more support for it than is commonly realized. One of the more dramatic illustrations of this support has been the evolution of public opinion toward the guaranteed income. Rejected in the early sixties by almost everyone as a dangerous innovation which would destroy the basic industrial-era philosophy, it is coming to be understood as essential.

As we move toward an insurance societal security system, we must face up to the fact that the Topsy-like growth of the present elements of our insurance societal security system has led to gaps and overlapping. Farmers usually receive more help than those poor people who live in cities. Those who are unemployed usually get more resources if they have recently held jobs than if they have not. What we need now is a *system* which is expressly designed to provide resources to *all* those who need them.

The key word here is "system." Our technique for providing resources must be systematic rather than partial, for otherwise we shall be forced to continue with the neo-Keynesian system despite its unsatisfactory nature. What, then, are the necessities?

1. We must find ways to provide sufficient resources to permit

individuals to live with dignity. This means the provision of a guaranteed income—or, as I prefer to call it, Basic Economic Security (BES), which will be adequate without supplementation by a job.

BES would be tax free. All money received from any other source would be taxed at an initial rate of, say, 35 percent. (Other taxation issues are considered in the next chapter.) The 1969 welfare reform proposal of President Nixon therefore fails to meet our real needs. It creates a scheme which is based on the assumption that jobs will continue to be available to all. We are, therefore forced deeper into neo-Keynesian policies and all the dangers already described.

2. BES would meet the needs of those who were unable to obtain a well-paying job even during the period when the neo-Keynesian system was still fully operative.

A second problem arises, however, as one contemplates the effects of a deliberate decision to end pressures toward full employment. It is then inevitable that some of those now earning higher incomes would find themselves unable to obtain jobs. What should we do for such people? We can take two stands. We can argue that as their higher incomes stemmed largely from past uses of power, there is no obligation for the society to provide anything more than a basic income to those who lose higher paying jobs. Alternatively, the society can decide that it is both wise and just to cushion the income shock and the psychic costs involved in the loss of a well-paying job.

There is considerable evidence that the life styles presently demanded of middle-income individuals commits them to levels of expenditure which leave them with little free money. A decision to make middle-income individuals who lose their jobs live on BES would force them to abandon their whole existing way of life. This would have three undesirable consequences:

1. In economic terms, it would mean radical changes in demand

patterns and major dangers of local, or total, economic depression.
2. In political terms, it would develop the already-evident drive toward a neo-Luddite revolt as well as increase the support for reactionary political movements.
3. In systematic terms, it would lead to a sharp income division between job holders and those who do not hold jobs. This would greatly complicate the necessary task of communication between the two categories.

We therefore require the development of Committed Spending (CS), a societally backed insurance scheme based upon previous earnings. In effect, an individual would obtain vested rights to income over a period of years on the basis of his declared tax income each year. The total income received under CS would, however, be no more than a given multiple of the amount available under BES and policies should be so arranged that CS entitlements should decline toward the BES level over time.

There are other issues involved in the distribution of resources. We must provide people with ways of obtaining a good education, adequate health care, and a method of insuring against major loss. It seems probable that the educational system should evolve in the direction of greater flexibility, with each individual receiving funds that he can spend for either private or public education. It seems that our health systems must evolve from insurance to guaranteed care: that we must change the medical structures so that inefficiency and poor care cause financial penalties rather than advantages—the latter being the effect under many present insurance schemes. Systems for covering catastrophic loss already exist, of course, although modification of many of them (for example automobile insurance) is urgently required.

In the insurance societal security system that is necessary for the future, income is distributed as a right; pressures to hold a job are not desirable, or indeed possible. The immediate reaction to this statement is, of course, how will the society function without incentives? We have already given a partial answer to the objection, but we must now examine it in more detail. It is commonly assumed that if a person is not forced to work he will fail to do so. People therefore wish to preserve work incentives.

This technique will not be satisfactory, however, because of changes in the work to be done. In the past, the nature of the work required and the standards of performance could be clearly set. The person who did not do his well-defined job was fired. In the future, as structured, repetitive work is taken over by machines, more and more of the activities remaining for men will require creative judgment and action.

At this point, the relationship between an employee and his employer necessarily changes profoundly. So long as it was possible to provide people with a set task for the day or week and to judge the percentage of the task performed, an authoritarian system sufficed. It is today impossible, in a growing number of areas, not only to state *how much* should be done but also *what* should be done. Once we understand this, we perceive that work can be effectively carried out only if there is successful communication between employer and employee.

This is the reason why management has had to change from its previous hierarchical style. It is also the reason why new patterns of incentives must be found. Incentives based on fear of being fired or hope of promotion are ineffective—indeed dangerous—in a communications-based system. People who are afraid of losing their jobs or who concentrate on insuring their own future will distort the truth to please their bosses; the accurate feedback required for effective decision making cannot occur.

The only feasible incentive pattern for a communication era appears to be a very old one: man's faith in his own capacity, his willingness to stand up for what he believes to be right, and his courage to change his beliefs when he is proved to be wrong. One of the most tragic elements in our current situation is our unwillingness to encourage those who do possess and practice these qualities. We end up, all too often, firing the individual who has placed his feedback responsibility above his loyalty to his boss. It is at this point that we discover that the rhetoric of management and its realities still all too often diverge. Managements often call for accurate feedback to insure effective decision making, but when they obtain it they usually react negatively.

OTHER POLICY MEASURES: LABOR-MANAGEMENT, CAPITAL, TAXATION

The last chapter discussed what new policies should be developed to change the distribution of resources. This chapter will examine other necessary, parallel policy changes.

LABOR- MANAGEMENT RELATIONS

At the present time, strong labor unions can obtain wage increases far above the rate justified by increases in productivity. In recent years, weaker labor unions have done far less well, and some unorganized workers have actually suffered a decline in their standard of living. Similarly, large marketives have increased their profits, while smaller, less powerful marketives have often been in severe difficulty.

Large unions reached their present position of power after Western societies perceived how weak the bargaining possibilities of the working man were compared to the marketives which he confronted. When this was understood a series of measures was passed to provide unions with the power to confront marketives, and particularly large corporations, on more equal terms.

The inevitable result followed. When unions and marketives came to possess relatively equal power, fighting was unsatisfactory, for it cost both sides heavily. Both groups soon discovered that it was also often unnecessary. Given neo-Keynesian policies, it was possible to provide workers with the increase in income they demanded and then to pass on more than the full cost of the rise in wages to the public, thus insuring increased profits.

Even when there is an initial failure to agree between marketives and unions and a strike does result, the costs are seldom borne by the unions and marketives themselves. At the end of strikes, marketives typically find themselves confronted with a backlog of demand which can only be worked off by employing workers overtime; workers therefore make up most, or all, of their lost wages. The marketive also promptly raises prices at the end of the strike, not only on new production but also on ecofacts produced before the strike, thus insuring that it limits or eliminates its losses and passes on the additional costs to the purchasing public.

The financial aspect is only part of the overall cost to the public. The granting of the right to strike to the union and the right to lock out workers to marketives was based on the belief that management and labor would struggle against each other. Today, labor-management struggles usually involve the public more or less directly. Strikes of taxi drivers and telephone workers, airline employees and railroad men, educators and policemen hurt the public by making it more costly to earn a living, by disrupting plans, and so on. As we move still further into a service economy, the costs of strikes to the public will be ever more direct and ever higher.

There is an additional systematic cost which must be taken into account. As man gains power to alter the world in which he lives, he needs ever-better communications to insure accurate feedback and effective decision making. Strikes and lock outs damage communication patterns, and, indeed, threaten the technological infrastructure on which the functioning of the socioeconomy is now based. We cannot afford to make communication more difficult than it inherently is.

The position of the public has changed; the attitudes and actions of unions and marketives are under increasing attack. Excessive wage and price increases, coupled with disregard of the public interest, have created pressure for new legislation which will reduce the power of marketives and unions to obtain larger shares of the increase in resources than are justified. This pressure, however, is likely to have very unequal results, unless we recognize that the power of marketives is far less vulnerable to legislation than the power of unions. The present power position of unions was created by legislation which can be reversed. The position of marketives is inherent in their structure; it has been little affected by policies such as anti trust and similar legislation. The likely direction for anti-union legislation are the abolition of the closed shop, which forces workers to belong to unions.

In more general terms, compulsory arbitration may well be introduced when a strike would directly affect the public or the public interest. In considering such strikes, there should be no confusion with the issue of whether the employee is hired by a public or private organization. We shall need to go further, however—to move toward Swedish patterns, where there is a continuing and largely successful attempt to gain societal agreement about the proper distribution of the additional resources which become available.

FINANCIAL CAPITAL

The crisis in the union-marketive field is increasingly obvious and increasingly noted. The crisis over rights to resources achieved by ownership of capital is not yet really understood or even perceived. We have never faced up to the implications of the fundamental changes which have occurred in the rights of the lender and the borrower throughout the period of the industrial revolution.

Until the mid-nineteenth century, the risk of the lender was usually complete. If an individual lent money to a commercial venture, he was normally forced to engage his total wealth. If the venture succeeded, he could become wealthy; if it failed, he had to satisfy all the creditors of the venture even if this meant bankrupting himself.

This situation came to prevent industrial expansion. Individuals had to be very careful where they placed their resources. Participation in most enterprises meant the risk of financial disaster if the enterprise should fail. People were therefore unwilling to lend freely enough to insure economic growth and it became clear that continued expansion would only be possible if the individual were permitted to control the extent of his risk. This result was achieved by the passage of the laws limiting liability. Under these laws, an individual's risk was restricted to the amount of money committed to the marketive; usually this meant the amount paid for the stocks or shares, although in some cases there were limited additional sums which could be "called" if they were needed to satisfy creditors.

At this point, the risk to the individual of lending money changed dramatically: he could now risk only a portion of his resources. In the new conditions, his risk was limited but his potential for gain was largely unlimited; the pattern of advantage had shifted dramatically in favor of the lender. This result was, however, not immediately perceived, for the life of marketives was still generally short and individuals still often lost all the money they had lent.

Late in the nineteenth and early in the twentieth century, conditions changed again. A group of stable marketives emerged. The risk of lending to marketives of this type was very small, for it was increasingly unlikely that such marketives would fail. At this point, therefore, lenders could choose their investments so they would be unlikely to lose money.

The final major shift in the degree of risk took place with the adoption of neo-Keynesian policies in the abundance regions. In effect, economic growth became guaranteed and the risk of the lender dwindled to minimal levels in lending to established marketives. Not only would the marketive to whom the individual lent money usually survive, but it was also very probable that, apart from short-run fluctuations, it would grow and provide higher payments.

The present, very large difference between the magnitude of risk and that of available reward is effectively disguised by the fact that since the original lender does not hold onto the shares he bought throughout the marketive's life, the gain of any one holder appears limited. However, this is not the relevant calculation. We should examine the payment made on a share from the time it is issued for so long as the marketive exists; this measures the total reward. In the case of many marketives, this reward is absurdly disproportionate to the original risk: the consequent excessive return to capital limits the return to labor and management and/or raises costs.

We must now distinguish between lending to a nonestablished marketive and the purchase or transfer of stocks and shares of established low-risk corporations on the major stock markets. We can first consider what should be our reaction to those who buy and sell the stocks and shares of established marketives and then go on to examine the appropriate methods of rewarding those who take major risks in providing funds to new marketives with uncertain futures.

It is still usually argued that those who lose or win money on the stock market are entitled to societal favor, for they take risks.

Each year some people who play the stock market end up gaining money while others lose it. There is certainly individual risk, but we must distinguish this from the long-run risk of the total "class of lenders"; i.e., all those involved in stock-market activities. The type of individual gain and loss inherent in playing the stock market must be described as equivalent to any other form of gambling: any particular transfer of shares between two people has no significant effect on the position of the marketive whose shares are traded.

Indeed, the gambling is not even fair: the stock market is "fixed" in favor of those with access to accurate information against those who fail to obtain it. (This does not mean, of course, that the pure gambler cannot do well but only that he is playing against the odds.) Increasingly, profits on the stock market come from early, privileged access to information. Such a situation is, of course, fundamentally unjust; the small investor is unlikely to do well. The classic statement that the odd lotter—he who buys or sells small numbers of shares—usually acts against the direction of the market is only one proof of this statement.

The present stock-market pattern must be changed because of an emerging clash between its method of operation and the necessity for accurate information movement. It is generally agreed that the stock market functions effectively, because it serves to balance *conflicting* views about the future of the economy, the future of various sectors of the economy, and of various marketives. The function of compromising divergent views about an uncertain future is always essential, but the methods used by the stock market are not appropriate in a communications era.

The stock market is so set up that it can only operate so long as a conflict of views exists; it is this conflict which provides stability. If general agreement should develop, prices of stocks and shares would rise and fall very sharply as everybody tried to buy at one time and sell at another. These rapid rises and falls in price would be less and less related to the actualities of the operation of the economy, and they would have a highly destabilizing effect: even the initial processes toward this pattern, as managers of growth funds have jumped in and out of the market together, have proved deeply disquieting.

Why should we assume, however, that there is any possibility of less conflict in views about the economy, about particular industries and particular marketives in the future than in the past? There are two factors which have already emerged and one which is inherent in the argument of this book. First, as a result of the development of the computer, information can be made more generally available. So far, the benefits of computer information systems have been limited by problems of information overload and restricted circulation patterns, but these situations can be expected to change. Second, the Securities and Exchange Commission is demanding increasingly that methods of limiting information to certain clients or classes of clients be eliminated. As a consequence of the better and more complete information flows resulting from these two forces, we can expect those playing the stock market to reach similar conclusions at the same time, thus increasing stock-market fluctuations in particular marketives and industry groups.

In addition, it is obvious from the argument of this book that there will have to be far greater agreement on appropriate and probable directions for the economy if we are to be able to insure accurate feedback and effective decision making. This, in turn, will tend to lead to exaggerated upward and downward movements of *all* the stocks and shares on the stock market.

In effect, the obsolescence of the stock market is one of the inevitable effects of changing from a society which is believed to move in the right direction because of an Adam Smithian competitive hand to a society in which we know that the future must be planned through cooperative action. In the society of the future, we must get rid of as many sources of built-in disagreements as we can. The stock market, as presently structured, requires *disagreement* in order to function. There is therefore no place for a stock market of the present type in the communications era.

The stock market's function as a buyer and seller of existing stocks and shares is therefore obsolescent. This is not as shocking a statement as it may appear to many at first sight. The buying and selling function of stock markets was always intended to be a means to the end of permitting effective money raising for marketives in need of resources. It was correctly argued that people would not buy stocks and shares unless they could dispose of them without excessive loss if they wished, or were forced, to do so; the stock market developed for this purpose.

As occurs very frequently, the means has since become an end in itself; this end can now be seen to be undesirable. Enormous amounts of time and effort are spent to promote the buying and selling function of the stock market.

Granted that one of the key shortages is now, and will be, that of creative and imaginative people, we must discover new ways to make stock transfers and to raise money for established marketives. Far simpler mechanisms than those which presently exist would suffice for this purpose.

We must also deal, however, with the highly complex question of providing funds to those new marketives which have the potential of producing desirable ecofacts. All too often, at the present time, it is easier to obtain money if one knows the right people than if one possesses the necessary skills. As we urgently need new ideas, we must develop more imaginative methods of providing risk capital; it will be useful here to consider risk once more.

The provision of risk capital implies that the lender is prepared to lose his money; that only some of the marketives he backs will pay off. Nevertheless, because his potential for loss is never unlimited, he should not have the right to unlimited gain.

The key to a restructuring of risk and interest rates is a fundamental rethinking of our attitudes toward risk on capital. We have discovered as a society that certain rates of interest are grossly excessive, and we have tried to alter the situation by such bills as "truth in lending." No substantial changes are going to occur, however, until we understand that what we commonly call "the rate of interest" contains three elements: compensation for risk, administrative and other expenses, and interest itself. We should pass legislation requiring that these three elements be stated separately.

The element of risk should be stated in terms of the estimated possibility that the borrower may default in paying back his loan or that a marketive may be unsuccessful. In some cases, the risk element can be computed on the basis of past experience—for example, it is known that the risk of default on consumer loans is low. In other cases, the estimate of risk must necessarily be highly subjective; it then seems reasonable that the appropriate degree of risk premium should be established by competitive bid. The lender who demanded the smallest guarantee against the risk involved in lending to particular marketive would obtain the right to make the loan. Having made the loan, he would then possess, in addition to stocks of the marketive, risk certificates which could be traded on the open market.

Let us suppose that the lender agrees to provide $10,000 to the marketive at a 2 to 1 risk premium: i.e., for every $1,000 he lends he is entitled to receive $2,000 in risk premiums. In this situation, the borrower receives $10,000 in cash, and the lender receives $10,000 in stock on which he will be paid the going rate of interest plus $20,000 in risk premiums. These risk premiums entitle him to receive a total of $20,000 from the future profits of the marketive. Once the $20,000 has been paid, however, no more money will be paid by the marketive to compensate for the initial risk involved in lending the money.

These risk premiums should be traded on the market and sold separately from the stock with whose issue they were originally associated. The value of a risk certificate will depend on the estimate of those involved in buying and selling risk premiums of the probability of the marketive paying off outstanding risk premiums and the amount of time it will take the marketive to do so. As the marketive becomes more successful, the value of its risk premiums will rise.

Marketives will try to pay off risk premiums as rapidly as possible, for their cost of raising additional money in the future will depend largely on the amount of risk premiums outstanding. If the marketive has been successful in paying off previous risk premiums, the premiums involved in the next borrowing will be smaller. If it has been unsuccessful, its payments for risk premiums will be higher.

While it has become inappropriate to trade stocks of established companies because of the lack of uncertainty involved, it will be valuable to continue to trade risk certificates for as far ahead as one can see. The significant differences in opinion which are required to make a "market" possible are inevitable in the case of new marketives.

The level of present charges for borrowing and payments for lending do not appear to have caught up with the implications of the present inherent guarantee of perpetuation of all large marketives. It is no longer possible for the government to permit the collapse of the economy or any large part of it. The size of the differential in payments on governmental and industrial stocks therefore seems excessive in many cases.

The statements made above should not be seen as a denial of the possibility of a total collapse in the economic system; it seems increasingly clear that such a collapse could occur if we fail to understand the new economic problems and possibilities which confront us. *I am stating only that if such a collapse should occur, government bonds would be essentially as vulnerable as the bonds of large corporations.* The total socioeconomy is now inextricably linked into a single whole; public and private functions can no longer be untangled.

Once we have separated out the risk element involved in lending, any remaining differentials between payments to different lenders and charges to different borrowers can only be justified on the grounds of varying administrative charges and other costs. It is obviously true that the small borrower and lender entail larger percentage costs than the large; however, it is essential that these costs be separately stated and not hidden in an overall "rate of interest." It may well be that we shall discover that with the coming of the computer and subsequent reorganization, costs for handling small lending and borrowing transactions can be substantially reduced.

The actual rate of interest, excluding risk and necessary charges, should be the same for every borrower. There is no reason why a large lender should receive a higher rate of interest than a small one or a large borrower should benefit from a lower rate of interest than a small one. Once legislation requires that rates of interest be stated separately from risk premiums and costs, it will be possible to discover which borrowers and which lenders are benefiting unduly and which are being treated unfairly.

The requirement for the same basic interest rate for all borrowers and lenders, exclusive of risk and costs, will eliminate the feasibility of much speculation. It will, in effect, prohibit the issuance of common stocks and only permit the sales of fixed-interest securities.

The classical objection to fixed interest securities—that they do not provide enough potential for gain to encourage people to invest in risky stocks—has been met in so far as it is in the public interest to do so. Any individual can choose to invest in an enterprise of any given degree of risk, and if his judgment is correct, he will obtain the risk premium he thought he needed to make the investment worthwhile. He will, however, no longer be able to obtain unlimited payments for limited risk.

In what direction can we expect the rate of interest to move in coming years? Much has been made of the rapid rise in interest rates throughout the world in recent years, but, in reality, interest rates have fallen in most areas. Interest rates should be considered net of inflation. The lender is interested in how much more his money is worth at the end of the year and not in how many dollars he receives. Basic interest rates in many parts of the world are still inadequate to compensate for inflation. Increasing sophistication about the implications of inflation will necessarily push interest rates to even higher levels until inflation is controlled.

When we end neo-Keynesian policies and substitute for them policies designed to change the distribution of income, deflation will take the place of inflation. The long-run trend for interest rates will therefore be downward as we come to understand the need for fundamental change in economic theory and practice.

TAXES

Like every other part of the socioeconomic system, our methods of levying taxes grew without plan. Indeed, we have never really been comfortable about levying taxes at all, because neoclassical theory "proved" that we were interfering with a fair distribution of resources based on contribution to production.

It would be impossible to list all the motivations which have affected the development of Western tax systems, but four of the most important should be noted.

1. We have felt that the rich were most capable of paying taxes, but we have tempered actions based on this belief because it was argued that: a. the rich deserved their income; b. the rich contributed more money toward capital formation, a process essential to economic growth in the early stages of the industrial era and one which is still considered essential.
2. We have felt we should limit the burden on the poor, but we have tempered actions based on this belief because it was argued that: a. the poor should pay for benefits received, as in the case of social security, local services, etc.; b. we have found that some of the easiest taxes to levy—for example, payroll taxes and sales taxes—have their heaviest proportionate impact on the poor.

3. We have used the tax system as a means to promote desirable economic and, increasingly, social goals and also to discourage "undesirable" activities.
4. We have felt an obligation to eliminate "injustices" when they have been perceived, and to cushion the impact of expenditures (such as those for illness or property loss) which could not be avoided.

We have succeeded in creating a mess. We have a crazy-quilt set of tax provisions, where total honesty becomes more and more difficult with every tax-reform bill because the legislation lacks clarity. In addition, many decisions are now made in terms of their effect on taxable income; tax advantages rather than the creation of desirable new ecofacts dictate many decisions. In consequence, the present tax system is a prime source of distortion to accurate feedback and effective decision making.

This is not the only reason for abandoning our existing tax system. There are few who would claim that it actually produces justice. Study after study shows that the percentage of income paid in taxes by the poor is high, that it declines for those in middle-income groups, and then rises again for the rich. However, the annual percentage paid in tax by the rich in the United States does *not* greatly exceed the percentage paid by the poor.

The time has come to develop a much simplified tax system. This becomes possible as soon as we have accepted the need for Basic Economic Security (BES) and Committed Spending (CS). Given the existence of a guarantee of income to all the population, we are able to abandon almost all the motivations which have led to the complication of the tax system.

BES would be tax free. All income above the BES level would be taxed at a rate of, say, 35 percent. Deductions would be at source for all wage, salary, or other payments. The 35 percent would cover present social security taxes, which would be abolished, and all federal income taxes. There would be no deductions and no exemptions except those necessary for earning one's income.

CS payments would be taxable. Earned and unearned income would be treated identically. Effective insurance schemes for education, health, and property would be set up; there would be no necessity to cover these factors through deductions from income tax.

Progressivity would be introduced into the tax structure at a suitable level, say at $15,000. The highest tax percentage should probably be no higher than 60 percent. As it becomes necessary to reduce the level of income inequality in order to balance supply and demand, we must alter the capacity to distort information to create artificial scarcity rather than attempt to compensate for excessive power through the income-tax mechanism. The move toward income equality must be achieved by fundamentally changing power relationships, rather than by trying to change the undesirable effects of power imbalances after the fact.

THE END OF INFLATION

Most economists today would agree that inflation is bound to continue into the indefinite future. They would support this view by an appeal to history, which shows a continuing decline in the value of money over time. They would also argue that supply is unlikely to keep up with demand in coming decades.

This general belief will be challenged here. *It will be argued that an understanding of systematic thinking, coupled with the development of accurate information movement, will inevitably force deflation.* The elimination of the power to create artificial scarcity, plus the introduction of BES and CS, necessarily implies a reduction in wages, salaries, and prices.

In order to clarify the issues raised by inflation and deflation, we must first examine the nature of these processes, for there is considerable confusion about them and about their significance. First, there are many problems in the calculation of the rate of inflation or deflation. It would be possible to state the alteration in the value of money unambiguously only if we lived in a totally static world without any changes. As soon as there are changes, all sorts of uncertainties are introduced: we are back to the problems caused by the flexibility of our measuring means. Products improve in quality, or they are made less well. Packaging changes in order to preserve perishables better. Distribution routes alter for the convenience of the marketive or for the convenience of the customer. There are no fully satisfactory ways of dealing with such changes; announced rates of inflation are approximate rather than exact. (It is often argued that an official annual inflation rate of 1 to 1½ percent actually means that no significant change is taking place in the price level.)

Deprived of emotional overtones, "inflation" describes the process by which the amount of money required to buy a certain quantity of ecofacts increases; "deflation" describes the process by which the amount of money required to buy a given quantity of ecofacts declines. Inflation tends to increase economic growth somewhat and deflation to discourage it; a growing economy is possible in either deflationary or inflationary conditions, so long as rates of inflation or deflation do not become excessive. The highly emotional connotations attached to both terms are largely undeserved.

As inflation has been the long-run state of mankind, as well as the predominant problem of Western industrial-era systems, we shall examine its causes first. We shall then go on to show that the policies proposed in the last two chapters will change conditions sufficiently so that we can anticipate deflation in coming years.

Economists have distinguished between two types of inflation. First, they have described the inflations caused by unions obtaining larger wage increases than are justified by rises in productivity and by firms increasing prices at excessive rates. Second, they have discussed the inflation caused by the government controlling the economy in such a way that too much money is available to the public. However, if neo-Keynesian policies are in effect, this distinction is not really useful, for the government can only restrain excessive wage and price increases by refusing to provide money to make them possible. This, in turn, would force the recession that neo-Keynesians are pledged to avoid. In a neo-Keynesian situation, inflation is inherent. It will not be controllable by the government until neo-Keynesian policies are abandoned. (I am assuming here that wage and price controls have been excluded from consideration because they directly distort feedback and cause major long-run dangers.)

Let us now consider what will occur if we adopt the policies described in the previous two chapters, which were based, in turn, on the analysis in the first part of the book. We can expect three major consequences. First, marketives and unions will begin to lose their power to distort information and to raise prices and wages by creating artificial scarcity. Second, the ending of neo-Keynesian policies will insure the freeing of large numbers of workers who presently hold jobs but do not contribute to the marketives or other bureaucracies. Third, the availability of BES and CS will provide an alternative form of income for people, and some will use the consequent freedom to create new organizations producing different ecofacts.

ELIMINATION OF POWER OF UNIONS AND MARKETIVES

The creation of policies designed to limit the desire and power of marketives and unions to distort information and to raise wages and prices by creating artificial scarcity will diminish the major present pressure toward inflation in Western industrial-era systems. At this point, the society will be able once more to make decisions about the ways in which increasing resources *should* be distributed.

In effect, the rate of introduction of BES and CS will have to be determined by the availability of funds: the larger the rate of increase in yearly supply, the more rapidly we can expect to achieve adequate levels of BES and CS. One of the major tasks of economic policy makers in coming years will be to regulate the pace of introduction of BES and CS. If the rate of introduction is too fast, we could re-create a demand-induced inflation. If the rate of introduction is too slow, we shall not create with sufficient rapidity the new *system* of income distribution which is necessary before we can eliminate neo-Keynesian policies.

END OF NEO-KEYNESIAN POLICIES

The constraint of neo-Keynesian policies can be restated very briefly. It has been assumed in Western industrial-era systems that each individual should be able to support himself. In present conditions, this means that the vast majority of the population must be able to hold a job.

When it is no longer necessary for the government to insure that everybody can find a job, conditions will change in many ways. Government policies will gradually shift away from their present shape, which has been created by the constraints inherent in neo-Keynesianism. Governments will come to admit their incompetence to retrain many types of workers. They will drop their support of social structures designed to promote the increase of demand. For example, we can expect a move away from road building as well as an increased concern for the rights of public, as opposed to commercial, television. At present, commercial networks do not pay for the channels that they use: there is no good reason why license fees should not be levied for the use of the public air waves. These fees could then be used to support public television. (There is no suggestion here that public television has so far been more imaginative and creative than commercial television; it is only being argued that we *must* learn how to use TV for effective instruction and that this cannot easily be done within a commercial, demand-inducing framework.) In effect, the whole fabric of Western society has been wrenched by neo-Keynesianism, and the process involved in growing beyond it will be extremely far reaching.

At the same time as governments abandon many policies and adopt new ones more suitable for the communications era, marketives will rethink their staffing patterns. They will start by firing those inefficient, uneducated workers who have been forced on them by public and governmental pressure. They will discover the extent to which Parkinson's Law and Peter's Principle have operated in management—and union pressure has operated on the factory floor—to prevent efficiency. They will perceive that large numbers of workers, at all levels, can be released without diminishing production. They will even find that in some cases production increases as the work force is reduced. The apparently surprising statement that production may increase with a diminishing work force is based on the fact that inefficient workers now often have a negative effect on production—not only because they may make mistakes but also because they take up the time of those who *are* efficient. For example, how many committees today are so designed that in effect they limit efficiency in decision making rather than enhance it? The release of large numbers of workers would obviously permit declines in prices of ecofacts.

This does not, of course, insure that a decline in the price of ecofacts will necessarily occur. Given present patterns of thinking, those who remain in their jobs will try to obtain larger increases in income than in the past; they will argue that they are responsible for all the productivity increase resulting from the elimination of the excessive work force. This argument is, of course, invalid; as we have seen, our ability to increase production emerges from the growing information in the society, which has been made available to men by education and has been incorporated in machine systems. In order to insure the development of the deflation which is made possible by the end of neo-Keynesianism, we shall have to understand fully the forces which are now operating. It is only in this way that we can make certain that we do not continue the policies which were necessary in a neo-Keynesian period but which are not suitable for the new economic conditions that will emerge.

It is important to restate at this point the costs of the end of neo-Keynesianism. We are capable of structuring patterns of resource distribution so that economic loss is limited. Unfortunately, however, we cannot avoid very severe individual psychic hardship, for the policies now necessary will inevitably seem undesirable to large parts of the population which were brought up to believe in older norms that are no longer applicable.

In order to prevent the growth of the most destructive feedback patterns, it must be made clear in all discussions of these topics that work will always be available for all. There will be a shortage of jobs but not of meaningful activity. The cybernetic revolution sets man free to act in more imaginative ways; it does not condemn him to idleness. Those with least formal qualifications often have the empathy required to do human service jobs well.

VOLUNTARY ACTIONS

We have dealt in the last section with some primary consequences of BES and CS linked with the ending of neo-Keynesian policies. We must now examine what will happen as people are provided with new freedoms to choose their own patterns of activity. The first concern of most Americans when confronted with the possibility of BES and CS is that everybody will quit work. It is this pattern which is most deeply feared and most often noted. Any discussion about increasing the degree of societal insurance in the culture leads to immediate fears that we shall generate a nation of bums.

We are generally less than logical on this issue. First, we ignore the overwhelming evidence that most people are unhappy doing nothing and that, particularly in Western cultures, there is a continuous search for meaningful activity.

Second, our concern about idleness is highly selective. We worry, as a banker once put it, about the 2 percent of bums among the poor and ignore the 2 percent of bums in all other income classes. If idleness and goofing off are sins worthy of denunciation, surely this remains true regardless of whether the individual is poor or wealthy? As we have seen, there is no proof that the rich "deserve" their wealth; they often receive their resources on the basis of their power rather than of their contribution. Indeed, even if this issue is examined most narrowly in terms of the cost to the taxpayer, it seems probable that the loopholes developed for the richer taxpayer cost as much as the payments to the truly poor.

Third, our definition of idleness is very narrow. We assume that people are not "worthy" if they depart from community norms. Indeed, it is still true that in many cases the mere lack of a job is enough to lead to a suspicion of idleness. As we face new problems and develop new patterns, it may well be that what we currently define as idleness will be of critical importance to our long-run development.

Finally, if the individual is really determined to goof off, he will do so. Society's only choice is to let him goof off by himself or to force him to goof off within the confines of an organization. The cost to society will be *very much lower* if the idler wastes only his time rather than involving that of men with potential for significant thought and action. The growing lack of structured activity today makes it impossible to force people to toil without incurring excessive social costs.

DEVELOPMENT OF CONSENTIVES

The time has come for us to be more concerned about the positive aspects of BES and CS than the negative. We need to study whether such measures will provide more opportunities to those who are capable of innovative changes. Once we turn the problem around in this way, we can begin to see the potential introduced by BES and CS.

The most serious weakness of our present economic and social system is its failure to support original work which has breakthrough potential. Today, as we try to move through the transition from the industrial era to the communications era, we urgently need new and creative ideas as well as people capable of implementing them. There are few institutional arrangements for this purpose today, and those that do exist are faulty.

It is now well known, for example, that a marketive which pioneers in a fundamentally new, and socially desirable, field often does not make the profits from it; these are obtained by others who take advantage of the pioneering work. In addition, the bureaucratic functioning of financial markets, which insures that they spend more time dealing with the transfer of existing shares than the finding of new money for worth-while enterprises, limits the resources available for new and creative activities. In another area, we know that support patterns for those doing imaginative basic research, particularly in the social sciences, are very imperfect. Grants are normally received by people who have skills in writing proposals and in standing well within their professions, rather than by those who have the capacity to carry out creative work.

As we saw in the previous chapter, we faced a similar effective limitation on socially desirable enterprise in the mid-nineteenth century. Those who invested in a firm or corporation were liable to the total extent of their wealth if there was financial failure. Under these circumstances, people were unwilling to invest. We ended this restriction on enterprise by the invention of limited liability; an individual could then lose only the money he invested.

BES and CS will serve the same function for the immediate future as the institution of limited liability has done for the last hundred years. They will provide individuals and groups with the opportunity to work in those areas which seem critically important to them. The individual will not get rich while he chooses this approach, but at least he will have the guarantee of a minimal standard of living.

The most significant tasks now facing our culture cannot be accomplished within present organizations. The availability of BES and CS will provide the financial base which will permit people to take risks in developing new ecofacts that may be needed by the society. Many of the unfilled opportunities in our society require looser structurings and greater unity of purpose than are presently possible in most bureaucratic marketives. Creating new institutional forms to permit people to join together in new groupings for economic purposes will be critical for the future. These new groupings, therefore, deserve a specific name to distinguish them from marketives; I have suggested calling them *consentives*.

The essential difference between a consentive and a marketive is the motivation that holds the group together. Marketives are formed to make profits; social priorities must necessarily take a secondary place. Consentives, on the other hand, are formed around an agreed purpose; if this purpose turns out to be money-making as a secondary consequence nobody objects, but this is not the prime purpose. (If at any time the group changes its priorities toward money-making, the group changes from a consentive to a marketive.)

Consentives will therefore not only increase production, but they will also pioneer in developing new styles of organization. Consentives will invent the organizational forms required to permit effective changes in marketive priorities and organization.

Consentives which produce ecofacts will be particularly effective in bringing downward pressure on prices; their members will very often be willing to accept lower standards of living to do what is important to them. It should be noted, in addition, that consentives may discover that the medium of money is not a satisfactory method of controlling the exchange of the goods and services they wish to produce. In this case, they will move toward the creation of sociofacts—goods and services whose exchange is not mediated by money—and the creation of new social rather than economic forms. This pattern is considered in the epilogue.

Who will choose to leave marketives and enter consentives? The more dynamic and creative people will be attracted to the options resulting from BES and CS. Throughout history, it has been true that the most imaginative and energetic people leave existing structures and organizations when new possibilities emerge, while those who are content with existing, more limited, horizons stay.

This is the "pull" factor inherent in the new situation. But there is also a "push" factor: people will leave their existing jobs most frequently when these jobs are perceived as unpleasant. Unpleasantness, however, is a subjective quality: a job which one person would do under no conceivable circumstances, another person is totally unwilling to quit. There is, however, one situation which more and more people find intolerable: this occurs when their creativity and imagination are constrained by the structural authority of bureaucrats.

The movement of the most effective people out of the most unpleasant jobs will force change on marketives, other bureaucracies, and on the total social structure. Marketives and other bureaucracies which find their most imaginative and creative people leaving will be forced to improve their attractiveness in order to try to hold their best workers. While higher salaries may have some effect on the level of attractiveness, it will increasingly be necessary to insure relevance in each individual's activity. It is this process which will force the marketive toward the style of the consentive.

The shift in the social structure due to consentives will be far reaching. It will be particularly obvious, however, in the selling sectors of the economy. A large percentage of the imaginative people working in advertising, public relations, and other promotional jobs stay in them only because they see no viable alternative. When BES and CS develop many of the most creative people will leave their jobs. As a result, advertising quality will decline. This will lead to increased pressure for the elimination of commercial clutter and more direct concentration of program quality.

**THE CAUSES
AND CONSEQUENCES
OF DEFLATION**

We have identified three forces which are likely to bring about deflation. First, the end of neo-Keynesian policies will limit the power to create artificial scarcity. Second, it is possible to free a very substantial proportion of those working in marketives and bureaucracies, with consequent reduction in costs and taxes. Third, the creation of consentives will lead to effective downward pressure on prices, as people work for their own pleasure rather than primarily to make money.

We can also state this issue in general theoretical terms. We saw in the first chapter that the cost of any ecofact varies with supply and demand; as supply rises, price tends to fall. The same rule holds true for a situation in which the supply of most desired ecofacts rises: the overall price level will tend to decline. This result has been avoided in recent years only by a concerted effort of all those in the economy to block normal feedback channels. As we eliminate the barriers to feedback, the results normally to be expected will occur.

What are the implications of deflation? We must look at this question in two areas: first, consequences for the distribution of income and second, consequences for the rate of economic growth. We must be careful, however, not to argue about whether deflation is good or bad, it is inevitable because of our necessity for accurate information movement. We can only ask whether there are any favorable consequences which can be enhanced and unfavorable consequences which can be avoided.

Who benefits when the cost of ecofacts declines during the process of deflation? Obviously, those who have saved money benefit. A worker who saved during his work life finds, when he retires, that his savings will buy more than when he invested them, even without considering interest payments. Those who saved during their work life are far better protected in deflationary conditions than in inflationary ones. This benefit of deflation also goes to the rich, but it seems certain that the benefit the rich achieve in this way will be more than offset by the decline in the power available to them.

Economists have usually argued that a condition of deflation was more just than a condition of inflation, because people would share more equally in the consequences of productivity increases. However, economists have been unwilling to promote the goal of a deflationary economy because they feared its consequences for economic growth; it has been proved that inflation tends to promote growth and that deflation tends to slow it. Given the neo-Keynesian commitment to growth, this was sufficient to make sure that economists would prefer inflation to deflation.

In effect, inflation encourages growth because it tends to "bail out" those who make mistakes. For example, if an individual opens a factory and produces ecofacts at a cost higher than that originally anticipated, the mere passage of time may enable him to sell them, assuming that the magnitude of his mistake was not too great. On the other hand, in a deflationary situation his overpriced stocks of ecofacts become less and less salable over time. This real impact on the salability of ecofacts which have already been produced is reinforced by a financial consequence. In inflationary conditions, the profits of marketives are increased, because the value of stock in hand rises as a result of inflation: profits thus appear higher than they actually are. Exactly the opposite pattern develops in deflationary situations: instead of "windfall" gains, the marketive suffers windfall losses, which reduce its profits.

SHORT-RUN ECONOMIC ISSUES

The dominant reality of the 1970s is that feedback channels, which have been artificially limited or blocked through many decades, are opening under the pressures which accumulated during the period of blockage. Because the channels have been closed for long periods, dangerous levels of frustration have developed, which must inevitably lead to severe clashes. Some of these clashes will occur between people who have perceived different parts of the blockage in feedback patterns—for example, the problems of poverty, environmental concerns, overconsumption, and so on. Those who have perceived a new issue tend to concentrate on those aspects of the overall situation which they have perceived most clearly, and will have different priorities for action. Other clashes will occur between those who have perceived the problems arising from blocked feedback channels and those who have not.

We shall deal with the consequences of some of the clashes in this chapter, but we must first face up to the fact that we are going to have to revise substantially our concepts of social justice and wisdom. In the past, those people who have been most successful in discovering new feedback channels have all too often felt justified in blaming others who were still trapped in older patterns of thought. Most people up to the present time have been forced to adapt to conditions, however unsatisfactory they might have seemed from a long-range point of view. The majority of the population had to live with conditions as they were rather than as they wished they were. They therefore had to act as intelligently as possible within existing conditions.

We have already seen that people were expected to be other-directed in the industrial era; it was assumed that they would follow the norms laid down for them by the society. People were not encouraged to seek ways to improve the overall situation. As we move into the communications era, we are changing the overall patterns encouraged by the society. We now demand that people become "part of the solution" to the issues we face. It is, however, unreasonable to fail to understand—and indeed sympathize with —those who were not brought up to see the potential for change but only the necessity for adaption. *We have always demanded adaption in the past; we must not blame those who learned the lesson taught by the society.*

We can see the implications of this reality most clearly if we return to the analogy presented in the second chapter. Those people who are forced to live in a room where the thermostat has been made ineffective by placing it in a refrigerator will suffer from excessive heat. In the short run, they will adapt by taking off as many clothes as they can within the existing definition of modesty. In the slightly longer run, the definition of modesty will change. In the long run, physiological mechanisms will come into play which make the body more comfortable at the heat level in the building; to a limited extent, changes of this type occur in every human being during seasonal weather changes. Finally, in the extreme long run there will be basic, irreversible physiological changes; the temperatures at which an Eskimo and a Bushman are comfortable are very different.

It follows from this analysis that the unblocking of feedback channels will inevitably lead to major disruption. Most people have been unaware of the blockage of feedback channels; they have therefore adapted to the conditions which existed. In a very real sense, the more intelligent the individual, the more successfully he will have adapted to present conditions and the more unfavorable may be the results of the unblocking of feedback channels for him.

Let us return for one final time to our analogy, and assume that the overheating has continued for so long that people have forgotten that the room was superheated by their previous standards. When they find the temperature of the room declining, they will actually feel change toward the previous norm as unsatisfactory and undesirable.

We can now apply this analysis to a specific problem—for example, that of pollution. As we become aware of the danger in which our environment has been placed, the society seems inclined to blame the industrialist. This is very largely unjust. The industrialist has been doing what the society demanded; he provided rapid growth in the supply of ecofacts. Neither he, nor the society perceived the real significance of the costs of pollution. It is therefore unwise and unjust to embark primarily on a campaign of punishing offenders. It was the total society that condoned the patterns of pollution, and the whole society must be prepared to pay the costs of its past failure. Industry alone cannot be expected to meet all the bill.

THE MAJOR FORCES AND MOVEMENTS OF THE SEVENTIES

We have identified throughout this book two major forces that are dramatically altering our ways of perceiving the economy. The first is the changing patterns of employment and unemployment, underemployment and overemployment. The second is the societal recognition that economic growth necessarily damages the environment.

Two new mass movements seem certain to emerge out of the realities of the job situation and the concern about ecology. One is a neo-Luddite revolt, aiming to destroy machines and machine systems and to limit the use of technology. This will be created by a fear of loss of jobs and a belief that the ecological crisis has emerged because of the use of technology rather than the misuse of technology. Even today, there is evidence of sabotage of machinery and slowing down of decisions; there is also a highly negative reaction to all forms of technology. The other movement will be a consumers' revolt resulting largely from a perceived need to restrict consumption in order to limit pollution, and from a changing psychological attitude toward the benefits of ecofacts.

What should the society's reaction be to these growing movements of the seventies?

The Neo-Luddite Revolt

The neo-Luddite revolt seems likely to have one good result: it will demythologize technology. Up to the present time, industrial-era nations, particularly America, have operated on the belief that anything which is possible should be done. The developing neo-Luddite revolt will certainly destroy this belief: it will force us to see that technology must be a means toward goals set on the basis of our values. I am not arguing, of course, that the certainty of this result would be enough to make the coming neo-Luddite revolt valuable. However, we are not dealing here with a social movement which can be averted if we so choose. The very most we can hope to do is to limit its magnitude.

Why should we struggle to prevent a neo-Luddite revolt from developing? The prime result of such a revolt would be to reduce the rate of economic growth; many people would consider this valuable at the present time. However, such a viewpoint ignores today's reality.

In our present culture, the largest part of the population still sees its satisfaction as being derived from a rising standard of living. Inability to provide this, as in recent years, leads to substantial discontent and tension. Such an atmosphere is not conducive to fundamental change, nor indeed to discussion of change. It is important to distinguish here between the necessary reaction to deflation and to the neo-Luddite revolt. Deflation does have a small unfavorable effect on economic growth, but it must be permitted to develop because it is the consequence of opening up feedback channels. The neo-Luddite revolt, however, is based on false premises: better patterns of information movement will undercut its development. Given a fundamental commitment to improve information flows, we can see why we must not try to prevent the development of deflation and why it is logical to try to prevent the extension of a neo-Luddite revolt.

The prevention of such a revolt is indeed of critical importance, for if it should develop to the extent which seems possible, we would be unable to introduce BES and CS with sufficient rapidity. While it is conceivable that people will give up a large part of any annual *increase* in production to others, it seems inconceivable that a large proportion of the population will accept, in the immediate future, a cut in their standard of living in order to finance the introduction of measures to change the distribution of income. In addition, we need rapid rates of growth to support greater help to the scarcity regions in the seventies. If the abundance regions do not act generously and creatively, tensions between the two may well grow to levels which would lead to the eventual destruction of the world.

A successful neo-Luddite revolt would therefore prevent any substantial increase in productivity and production. The consequent economic stagnation would make significant change impossible. Its supporters are, in fact, today's greatest reactionaries.

This conclusion is unexpected in the light of today's normal change strategies. It can, however, be generalized. It appears that the way to bring about change between one era and another is to keep existing systems functioning effectively until new ones have been put in their place. The strategies of change presently dominant are suitable only for struggles *within* one era; they can change the people holding power roles in the society, but they will not lead to changes in the definition and nature of power, which are critical in any move from one era to another.

The Consumer Revolt

A lead article under this title has already appeared in *Time*. The consumer has emerged as a political force: his actions are already significant. The question we must examine is the further direction of the consumer revolt and its potential for growth.

The consumer revolt has so far been concerned, in its most fundamental sense, with the task of ending the doctrine of *caveat emptor*—"let the buyer beware." The major drive has been to make marketives of all sorts responsible for the ecofacts they sell and service. This movement is gathering momentum, and it promises fundamental changes in the whole relationship between buyer and seller and the laws that govern purchasing transactions. In the past, marketives were held responsible only for actually stated guarantees. Increasingly, courts are deciding that the very act of sale implies a warranty as to the performance of the ecofact.

The direction of the consumers' revolt is clearly going to change significantly under the impact of ecological concerns. It is almost certain that the movement will go on to demand that ecofacts are made so that they will have optimal lives in order to minimize the waste of raw materials and the problems resulting from a throwaway culture. Those involved will become more and more interested in recycling; they will recognize that "waste" is simply a failure to recycle efficiently. This development will have considerable impact on marketive policies.

There is a further step in the development of the consumers' revolt which seems probable but which is not yet certain. This would emerge after we have become aware of the danger of overloading systems—particularly ecological systems. Each system is capable of a certain degree of self-cleaning or self-healing; if a system is overloaded it collapses.

As we perceive this reality for ecological systems, we are likely to come to understand the parallel for ourselves. More and more psychologists are already claiming that the basic problem of our culture is that of "overload"; people are receiving more information and stimulation than they can handle. It seems quite possible that a significant part of the population will be involved in a major movement toward the simplification of life and a decrease in the amount of desired ecofacts before the end of the seventies.

A considerable part of the activities of economists during the seventies will have to be employed in balancing the effects of the neo-Luddite revolt and the consumer revolt. This task can only be successfully carried through if we fully commit ourselves to creating an insurance societal security system. So long as we remain enamored of neo-Keynesianism, our problems will increase and could become insoluble: neo-Keynesianism will necessarily strive to prevent the consumers' revolt rather than to encourage it.

Can we, therefore, identify the major barrier preventing a commitment to an insurance societal security system? In the most general sense, it is the clash between the old and the new feedback patterns and also the clash between the various new feedback patterns. More specifically, one of the most dangerous patterns is our failure to separate the problems of overemployment and unemployability from that of unemployment. We must deal creatively with the overload burdening the most imaginative members of the society and with the lack of jobs for those who were only educated to work at structured activities. If we should fail to clarify this distinction, there will be increasing anger among those who feel they are being forced to overwork and increasing frustration among those who are unable to find jobs. In addition, the society will spend a large part of its time and energy trying to solve an unemployability problem which is inherently insoluble. Indeed the magnitude of the sixties attack on this diversionary issue has already had extremely serious results in preventing us from learning to move in more desirable directions.

Can we estimate the dates at which policy changes must be made if we are not to be trapped in increasingly difficult dilemmas? The timetable set out below is approximate, but it is included to demonstrate that we have run out of time in which we can stall. Somehow, in the near future, we must develop successful social, educational, and political means to bring about immediate fundamental changes.

1970–1971

Welfare reform with significant move toward BES.

1971–1972

Moves toward compulsory arbitration in the public interest along Swedish lines. The process begins of abolishing power granted to unions and marketives to distort information and create artificial scarcity so as to gain control of larger amount of ecofacts.

1974

Passage of legislation requiring that all lending and borrowing transactions state payments for risk, administrative costs, and rate of interest separately; payments for risk are limited in marketive-borrowing rather than totally open-ended. Movement toward single interest rate.

1976

Gradual introduction of CS. Fundamental tax reform over several years. (These two measures must probably be passed at the same time.)

1977–1979

Significant growth in consentives. Management of marketives changes its style toward that of consentives.

End of the Seventies

Societal commitment against all forms of information distortion.

I am aware that this timetable is "unrealistic." To those who raise this issue, I must answer in two ways. First, reform of the economic system is urgent now, and in its absence we can expect a growing degree of disruption. Second, there is some reason to believe that changes now come more rapidly than expected. BES, usually called the guaranteed income, was a poor joke when first introduced into discussion in 1962; we are now moving toward some form of guaranteed income in the near future. In another area, changes in public attitudes toward ecology in a single year show how rapidly views can alter and passions can be aroused.

We ended the introduction to our study of necessary policy questions by arguing that if one accepted the stated economic issue as real we would have to develop far faster and more effective means of bringing about change. Now that we have examined the magnitude of the requirements, it is useful to remind ourselves of the reality of our situation.

You, as reader, have three choices:

1. You can reexamine your initial acceptance of the posed problem/possibility and decide that it was not real.
2. You can accept its reality but deny the validity of the methods proposed in this volume for dealing with it. In this case you have a responsibility to develop better methods for yourself.
3. You can accept both the reality of the posed problem/possibility and, in general terms, the methods and the timetable proposed in this volume for dealing with them. In this latter case, two consequences follow.

First, societies must find some means of communication which are, at least, on an order of magnitude more effective than those in use today. Only in this way can we create public and legislative support for the necessary measures with sufficient rapidity.

Second, by the beginning of the eighties we shall have moved beyond economic concerns into socioeconomic. The epilogue that closes this book sketches some of the questions with which we shall have to learn to deal in the next decades. In addition, it discusses briefly the urgent problems of the scarcity regions which we have deliberately excluded from the rest of this book.

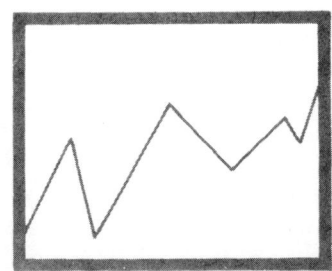

EPILOGUE

SOCIOECONOMIC PROBLEM/POSSIBILITIES

Our normal patterns of thinking are still profoundly static. We think as though we were confronted with disequilibria that intelligent action could eliminate once and for all. We still have not recognized that even if our actions were ideally suited to manage present problem/possibilities, new ones will inevitably emerge following our actions. Since neither our patterns of feedback nor our decision making are normally ideal, our actions will usually also create new disequilibria.

We must recognize that we are engaged in a constant cycle of feedback-action-feedback-action: each action changes the circumstances with which we are surrounded: these changes can then be perceived as the basis of the feedback. This feedback then enables us to act again, and so on.

The theoretical framework developed in this volume and the policies proposed for adoption would lead to highly significant changes in circumstances and in feedback. The purpose of this epilogue is to open up briefly some of the issues which lie beyond those treated in the body of the book.

We have already seen that the second part of this volume cannot be relevant unless the reader has accepted the conclusion that fundamental change in economic thinking and practice is urgently required. The issues taken up in this epilogue are even less relevant unless the commitment to fundamental change has been made.

I recognize, of course, the improbability of achieving this commitment in time to deal with the magnitude of the issues which confront us. "Rational" analysis of the present situation suggests that we will continue to act in ways which will destroy the carrying capacity of the earth. Brooding on this likelihood is, however, useless; in fact, it is likely to create the conditions for a self-fulfilling prophecy.

If there is to be any real possibility of changing our course with sufficient rapidity, our most urgent necessity is to discover those alterations in thinking and action which are required to permit us to enter the communications era. The body of this book has examined the short-run issues; this epilogue examines those which lie a little farther in the future.

It is, of course, impossible to discuss all the future problem/possibilities opened up by the argument of this book; severe selectivity is inevitable. We can start by considering the implications for the use of money which stem from the growing availability and increasing complex programming of computers. It is already accepted in banking circles that the use of cash will decline with great rapidity over the next decade, and that more and more exchanges of ecofacts will be based on the use of credit cards. Signs of the shift are already evident: a wider and wider range of purchases are made by credit card. For example, payment of certain taxes could be made on the basis of credit cards in 1970.

As is usual, however, the full revolutionary implications of this apparently evolutionary shift have not been perceived. There are two aspects of this development which deserve particularly careful attention. First, we must be concerned about the differential access to credit inherent in this development. Second, we must discover what will happen to the nature and meaning of money.

Credit cards were designed to make it possible to obtain ecofacts on the basis of one's signature rather than by immediate cash payment. The incentives leading to use in the early days of credit cards were convenient identification, effective record-keeping, and the additional time available for payment. As the number of sources issuing cards has increased, the scope of the credit available has broadened. The time permitted for payment has lengthened, the number of marketives participating has increased very rapidly, and, most importantly, an increasing number of credit cards now include as part of their services the availability of cash loans.

In effect, the ability to borrow money automatically has increased dramatically in recent years—for those who already have money. But these new sources of credit, like the old, are naturally almost entirely confined to the "credit-worthy." Those who have low-paying jobs, or whose employment record is faulty, find it just as difficult to get credit as in the past. As a result, the society is splitting between the credit-worthy and the noncredit-worthy.

It appears at first sight as though this split is merely a continuation of the old split between the rich and the poor. Such an assumption is incorrect, however, because of the formalization of systems introduced by the computer coupled with the job-destroying implications of the new technologies. We have seen that there will be an inherent tendency for the less creative and less imaginative to lose their jobs to machine systems in the coming decade. In a computer-based credit society, the loss of a job will usually entail the loss of credit-worthiness unless BES and CS have already been introduced. In the absence of BES and CS, therefore, the loss of a job will shift a family immediately and irreversibly from one style of living to another which is totally different and totally unwelcome. The hold of the employer over the employee would be dramatically increased, and the possibility of accurate feedback and effective decision making dramatically decreased.

This, however, is not the only change which will emerge as money transfers cease to be made on the basis of cash and are handled instead on the basis of information moved by computers. The availability of computers creates a profound difference in the methods of linking demand and supply. A primitive example of the developing pattern can be seen in the direct linkage of certain chains of stores to the factories that supply them, by the information which is coded on computer cards as each purchase is made. Each time an ecofact is sold, the purchase is recorded; detailed information is immediately available to the factory, which is able not only to replenish stocks on the basis of the feedback but which can also direct production on the factory floor with far greater efficiency than in the past. Management has available to it exact data as to the ecofacts which are found most attractive by the public. In these circumstances, a surprising degree of control has passed to the consumer. The very effectiveness of the communication link between store and factory gives far greater weight to his wishes. This process will inevitably develop further, for the computer will increasingly make it possible to design to the standards and wishes of the *individual* consumer. The possibilities in this direction have so far developed furthest in the case of the automobile industry.

This capacity to handle minutely detailed information has an unexpected result. Money used to be a common denominator for all transactions. While it was never fully satisfactory, it did provide an overall basis for judgment of trends. The growing availability and magnitude of computer capacity makes it possible to break data down again, thus avoiding the need for summing data into money terms—a process which never represented more than a first approximation to reality.

The trends created by this greatly increased ability to provide detailed information will be strengthened by the realities described in the body of the book. We saw there that ability to earn is not highly correlated with value, and need is not highly correlated with ability to pay. Inevitably, we shall be forced to accept that "money value" is *one form* of information to be considered in decision making, and not the *only relevant factor* as we often appear to believe today. In the future, instead of comparing the value of oil with the value of shoes on the basis of their rate of financial exchange, we shall be able to consider all the relevant factors—such as depletion of irreplaceable resources, employment of skilled personnel with alternative uses, costs in time and space, and so on.

In effect, money was an adequate linking mechanism so long as economists were concerned only with the relationships between production and consumption. We now need new measuring tools to discover both the worth of irreplaceable raw materials taken from the earth and the effort which should be made to recapture the wastes involved in production and consumption. A far more inclusive model is required which adds a fourth term, *resource reconstruction,* to the traditional three economic concerns of production, consumption, and distribution.

Mankind has created the potential for abundance. However, he can secure its continuing reality only if he takes two major further steps. First, he must spread the abundance not only to all those in the abudance regions but also to those in the scarcity regions. Second, he must recognize that the promotion and maintenance of abundance will be possible only on the basis of a fundamentally changed view of reality. We shall take up these two subjects in turn.

The reason we have not discussed the economic problems of the scarcity regions is because developing their economic potential depends on changes in thinking and policy in the abundance regions. In reality, most of the present "aid" from the abundance regions to the scarcity regions is not helpful. The abundance regions operate destructively, because they believe in a "stage" theory of human history, which was most clearly set out in W. W. Rostow's book, *The Stages of Economic Growth*. Rostow argued that each country and region must inevitably pass through the same stages. It follows that the scarcity regions can only achieve the present position of the abundance regions if they pass through all previous stages of economic growth faster than the abundance regions did.

Rostow's thesis is both politically unrealistic and intellectually naive. It is politically unrealisitc, because the present economic development of the scarcity regions is proceeding less rapidly than that of the abundance regions at the same stage of growth. If the scarcity regions should continue to pass through similar stages, the gap in wealth between the scarcity regions and the abundance regions will never close. This would necessarily lead to disastrous tension between the two and between the white and nonwhite peoples of the world.

Rostow's thesis is intellectually naive, because it assumes both that development is linear—i.e., that each country passes through the same stages of growth—and also because it is based on a thesis that the end point of human history is achieved as mankind enters the industrial era and benefits from the mass consumption made possible by it. Neither of these beliefs is correct. Countries have, in fact, made most progress when they have taken over the results of past experiences rather than duplicated the process which led to that progress. For example, Germany took over leadership of the steel industry by by-passing the British experience and immediately installing the most modern equipment. The belief of Rostow that human history ends with the industrial era has been proved to be incorrect in this volume. It is essential that we discover the pattern of the communications era which we must enter if we are to survive. We must therefore learn to make decisions on the basis of the actual situation in the agricultural regions today rather than basing our action on dubious parallels with the past.

Up to the present time we have transferred, without real thought, systems developed for industrial-era countries. We have failed to consider their degree of relevance in agricultural-era conditions. This has been true at all levels. It has been shown by our patterns of introducing new grains, by our choices of transportation techniques, by the relative importance given to transportation and communication expenditures, and by our insistence on certain patterns of management and politics.

It is not surprising, therefore, that the aid programs of the abundance regions have so far been relatively unsuccessful. Those planning further programs have, however, so far failed to perceive the significance of these failures. *They have claimed that the programs would have been successful if only the people in the scarcity regions had been intelligent.*

Aid programs will never be truly effective until we recognize that everybody in both the abundance regions and the scarcity regions always acts on the basis of his perceived self-interest. *Each individual will, when taking a decision, act in the way which appears most satisfactory to him given all the factors of which he is aware.* An alternative way to make this same statment is to argue that an individual will not take one decision if he is aware of another course of action which would be more satisfactory. There is, of course, no certainty that the individual's perception of his self-interest will be correct, but it is at least probable that those living in a situation will have a clearer perception of realities than most outside observers.

The issue involved here may become clearer if we look at the attitude of abundance region aid experts. A classic example of "stupidity" cited by experts is the unwillingness to adopt new techniques and materials which have been "proved" to increase production. This "failure" is, however, often highly rational in the light of real conditions in the scarcity regions. For example, let us look at the patterns which emerge as a new grain becomes available which doubles output in the normal year but which increases the risk of major crop failure by 25 percent. In a society of abundance it will make sense for the farmer to shoulder the extra risk to achieve the potential gain. However, a farmer living on the margin of subsistence may well find any extra risk unacceptable: crop failure would usually lose him his farm and sometimes cost him his life.

Because Western societies essentially believe that agricultural societies are inferior to them and must "catch up," they have shown little interest in creating knowledge specially suited for the scarcity regions or in finding new ways in which knowledge could be transferred effectively to those living in agricultural situations. This lack of interest continues, despite small-scale experimentation which has proved that people in agricultural cultures are capable of learning certain skills rapidly when their education takes place in appropriate ways.

One of the most severe barriers to help from the abundance regions is that Western man's attitudes were molded by literacy. Those who make educational policy are so blinded by this reality that they cannot imagine, much less accept, any full-scale system of transferring information which does not rely on writing and reading skills. International agencies and educational experts of both abundance and scarcity regions refused, until recently, to begin to test the hypothesis that radio, television, films, and so on, which by-pass the need for literacy can, in appropriate circumstances, be quicker and more effective ways of teaching and learning.

We can now perceive clearly why we cannot tackle the economic problems of the scarcity regions directly. Our present patterns of thinking dictate our patterns of action toward the scarcity regions. We shall inevitably continue to act in this way until we change our thinking. Thinking is rarely, if ever, changed except through an immediate crisis. The first task therefore is to convince those in the abundance regions that they need to change their *own* patterns of thinking. A significant change in thinking along the lines proposed in this book will inevitably improve the position of the scarcity regions in coming years.

This does not mean, of course, that we should cease to discuss the immediate problems of the scarcity regions, nor that we should give up the search for ways to speed the recognition of their urgent requirements. Let us look again at the issue of literacy: this may help to open our minds to their *real* needs.

We now have sufficient evidence with stressing the goal of literacy to discover that we cannot use this route to achieve the necessary massive transfer of information in the scarcity regions. The rate of population increase is so great that enough teachers cannot be made available: in addition, most of those who are taught enough to achieve literacy have so little opportunity to practice reading and writing after they leave school that their skills are rapidly lost.

Fortunately, the evidence is now so overwhelming that it is becoming impossible to ignore the educational realities of the scarcity regions. The developing feedback patterns are slowly but steadily overwhelming the shibboleths of the past. One example of the consequences of this realization is the decision by India to beam TV programs direct to villages via satelite.

What will be the consequences as scarcity regions recognize that they must move directly into the communications era without passing through the industrial era? Our failure to research, or even think about the process, leaves us with few certainties. We can only be sure that it is vital that the enormous power of the TV medium should be understood and respected. Its information-carrying capacity is so great that it will inevitably change fundamentally the villages it enters.

An even more dramatic issue lies ahead. We are now so accustomed to the relative failure of the scarcity regions that we assume, almost without thought, that this will certainly remain unaltered. We should, however, beware of any assumption that their past failures to achieve adequate rates of development will necessarily continue for the remainder of the century. The scarcity regions have been largely unsuccessful over the past twenty-five years because those from the abundance regions have managed to convince them that they should adopt industrial-era patterns. This approach was necessarily unsuccessful, because the scarcity regions had neither the capital, the skills, nor the cultural attitudes to permit them to move successfully from the agricultural era to the industrial era.

Once these regions recognize the need for a direct shift into the communications era, it seems possible that their basic cultural attitudes may actually be such that the transition from the agricultural era to the communications era might be remarkably smooth and swift. Many scarcity regions have cultural systems which recognize the virtue of cooperation. This emphasis on cooperation was a disadvantage in the industrial era, which was based on competition. The disadvantage changes into an advantage, however, once the nations in the scarcity regions recognize their need to enter the communications era which is based on accurate feedback and effective decision making; as we have seen, these are only possible in a cooperative society.

In the communications era, increased economic growth is not a goal in itself but rather the means required to achieve other goals. During the industrial era, man desired power to do everything. In a very real sense, the abundance regions reached a point where the ability to do something was sufficient reason to attempt it. In the communications era, when man has achieved the power to do anything that seems vital to him, his task is to discover which of the available opportunities he should attempt to pursue.

Cooperative systems, both in management and in the total culture, are the only effective ways to decide on future possibilities. Once a management group or culture has decided the directions in which it wishes to move, the availability of advanced machine systems will make possible any rate of economic growth that is necessary to achieve this goal without requiring the human competition which was necessary for this purpose in the industrial era. Such human competition was necessary in the industrial era, but it was also excessively wasteful: today our knowledge permits us to insure economic growth with rapidly decreasing hardship.

As a consequence of these developments, the relative advantage of the various areas throughout the world is changing fundamentally. Those countries which have entered the industrial era and adopted the competitive style have much to unlearn. This unlearning will always be difficult and will also tend to be partial; an interesting example of the failure to carry over new understandings to all relevant fields occurs as firms adopt the cooperative style for their own organization but continue to fight against moves toward cooperation in the total society.

It still remains true, of course, that only the abundance regions can provide the resources to permit the potential of the scarcity regions to emerge. They have a veto power over the possibility of development. We are therefore driven back once more to a recognition that the pattern in the abundance regions must change first. As we try to carry through this necessary task, we shall come to understand how deeply our faith in competition is woven into the fabric of our society. Perhaps the best brief way to drive home this lesson is to list some of the minimal necessities in a communications era:

1. We must develop a society based on sapiential authority (on knowledge), rather than on structural authority (on position). So long as power is based on structural authority, information will necessarily be distorted and accurate feedback and effective decision making is impossible. In a society based on sapiential authority, the social structure will inherently be open: people will rise on the basis of their competence in any

area that interests them. The extent of their rise will depend on their natural talents and, far more critically, on the amount of work they are prepared to do to develop them.
2. We must develop a society in which the concept of "nonzero-sum games" and "synergy" are firmly embedded. In other words, we must be able to understand situations in which all the participants in a situation gain by their involvement. Our key image today is that of the poker game where one player can win money *only* at the expense of another: this is a zero-sum game. We need to develop an image where the synergy inherent in intelligent interchange of ideas ensures that all those involved gain: this is a nonzero-sum game.
3. We must recognize that assumptions determine conclusions. Once we have decided on our assumptions, conclusions about appropriate actions can be deduced logically either by man or computer. This means that the present Western faith in objective analysis is challengeable like all other faiths: it amounts to a subjective claim that it is valid to exclude subjective aspects.
4. We must recognize that the dichotomized pattern of Western thought is inadequate to explain events in a communications era. Such dichotomies as bottom and top, good and bad are oversimplifications of highly complex perceptions. While we have no choice but to continue to use these dichotomies until we succeeed in developing new language patterns, we should always recognize that they disguise a far more complex pattern.

These issues are stated briefly because this is the end of a book and not the beginning. It is not, however, the end of the subject. Those who wish to move beyond the economic issues studied here can pursue these wider topics in two other volumes. In one of them, *An Alternative Future for America* (Swallow Press, Chicago), I have looked forward from 1970 to examine the nature of our present situation and the issues which we presently face. The other is *Teg's 1994: An Anticipation of the Near Future*, available from Personalized Secretarial Service, 5045 North 12th Street, Phoenix, Arizona 85014, at $5.00. Here my wife and I have looked back from 1994. We have described probable changes from the point of view of people living in many parts of the world who are interested in subjects such as ecology, education, politics, and communication.

These two books describe additional parts of the multifaceted reality which now confronts us. The usefulness of any particular description of reality depends, of course, upon the purpose for which it is designed and the people to whom it is addressed. For example, it is not appropriate to state that a particular table is made up of subatomic material similar to all other subatomic material if one is concerned with its qualities as a writing table or as an antique. It is equally inappropriate to describe the sheen of a table or the beauty of a flower if one is searching for the patterns which link all matter. To come closer to the subject of this book, it is not relevant to try to build a toal socioeconomic model if one started off by limiting oneself to a reevaluation of existing economics.

One of the problems we always face is that any depiction of reality necessarily depends upon the point of view: no description can be total. This book has tried to discover the ways in which economics can and cannot be used to clarify the nature of the situation which presently confronts us. It has therefore stayed as far as possible within the basic concepts and style of economics. The thrust of the argument in the volume shows, however, that we will necessarily be forced beyond economics in the very near future.

The valid truths of economics will inevitably be merged into an overall social-science theory. This theory is already in the process of creation: the main barrier to its rapid development is our continuing commitment to the survival of the various disciplines such as economics, sociology, and so on. We must move into a true transdisciplinary approach if we are to manage present and future problem/possibilities.